FRIEDRICH NIETZSCHE

BY

GEORGE BURMAN FOSTER

*Late Professor of the Philosophy of Religion
in the University of Chicago*

Edited by

CURTIS W. REESE

Dean of Abraham Lincoln Center, Chicago

Introduction by

A. EUSTACE HAYDON

*Professor of Comparative Religion in the
University of Chicago*

NEW YORK

THE MACMILLAN COMPANY

1931

SET UP BY BROWN BROTHERS LINOTYPERS
PRINTED IN THE UNITED STATES OF AMERICA
BY THE FERRIS PRINTING COMPANY

EDITOR'S PREFACE

THE late George Burman Foster (1858-1918) was one of the most towering and best known of the religious philosophers of the early part of the twentieth century. Born April 2, 1858, at Alderson, West Virginia, he was graduated from West Virginia University with an A.B. degree in 1883 and an A.M. degree the following year, having previously studied in Shelton College and having been ordained to the Baptist Ministry in 1879. On August 6, 1884, he married Mary Lyon, daughter of Professor Franklin Lyon of West Virginia University. In 1887, he graduated from Rochester Theological Seminary, and the same year became pastor at Saratoga Springs, New York, where he remained until 1891. During part of 1891 and 1892 he studied in the Universities of Göttingen and Berlin. Upon his return to America in 1892, Denison University awarded him an honorary Ph.D. From 1892 to 1895 he was professor of philosophy in McMaster University. From McMaster he went to the University of Chicago, where in 1895 he was made assistant professor of systematic theology, and in 1897 professor of systematic theology, a chair which he held until 1905, at which time he was made professor of the philosophy of religion in the Department of Comparative Religion, where he remained until his death. The publication in 1906 of his *The Finality of the Christian Religion* created a storm, the echoes of which still reverberate in Christian circles. This work was followed in 1909 by *The Function of Religion in Man's Struggle for Existence*. Deep in understanding and broad in scholarship, George Burman Foster shook the very foundations of orthodoxy and contributed in a large way to the present humanistic trend in religion.

It was natural for Professor Foster, himself of Zarathustrian spirit, to become interested in Friedrich Nietzsche and to interpret him generously. With careful, scholarly, critical insight he threads the maze of Nietzsche's remarkable personality, thought and career.

Few people have agitated the critical thought of the world more than Nietzsche, who vigorously and relentlessly waged warfare on what he regarded as the seven deadly evils—morality, socialism, democracy, feminism, intellectualism, pessimism, and Christianity. Bearing a name that literally means "the humble man," he became a champion of aristocracy. Hailing, as Doctor Foster shows, from generations of ministers and born in a parsonage, Nietzsche became one of the greatest foes of Christianity. Brought up by women, he became an antifeminist. Supreme egoist, he for a time became the devoted disciple of two masters, Schopenhauer and Wagner. Archenemy of nationalism and of pity, he went to the front as a war-time nurse.

Nietzsche cannot be understood without relating his writings to the different periods of his life. This Foster makes unusually clear. In his first period Nietzsche is the artist, justifying existence and the world as æsthetic phenomena. In his second period he is the positivist, the calm thinker, distrustful of art and metaphysics. In his third period he combines Schopenhauer's "will" with

EDITOR'S PREFACE

Darwin's "struggle" and "survival," and becomes the apostle of the Superman, in whose behalf all values are transvalued and to produce whom is man's one great end.

The work is a systematic and well-reasoned, appreciative study.

My own part in making possible this volume is so small and my debt to George Burman Foster so great, that I express all the more gladly gratitude to those who have joined in the work: to the late Mrs. George Burman Foster, who preserved the original manuscript; to George Herbert Clarke, of Queens University, whose editorial work on the manuscript was invaluable; to Douglas Clyde Macintosh, of Yale, who first submitted the work to Macmillan; to A. Eustace Haydon, of the University of Chicago, for his wise and penetrating introduction; especially to Mrs. Jennie Franklin Purvin of Chicago, former student of Professor Foster, who kept alive through weary moons the idea of publishing this book, and without whose interest and labors this work would hardly have gone to press.

CURTIS W. REESE.

Abraham Lincoln Center,
   Chicago.

INTRODUCTION

THESE lectures took form during the troubled years of the great war when the name of the lonely prophet of the *Ubermensch* was bitterly maligned and his teaching much misunderstood. It was characteristic of George Burman Foster to make this public plea for understanding. Though he concluded regarding life in more democratic terms than did Nietzsche there was much in experience common to these two men. Both knew the torture of spirit in wrestling in frank honesty with the problems of a world wrenched from its old, secure foundations on absolute truth. Both knew the sweet sadness of rejection by the good people still enfolded in untroubled security of church and creed. "I speak as a man who has suffered as keen spiritual anguish for twenty-five years as one could well suffer and maintain his sanity and health." These, Foster's words to his brethren in religion, would apply equally well to Nietzsche. Both men made the pilgrimage out of orthodoxy unable to find rest on any plateau of compromise until they set their feet upon the adventurous and uncharted path of pure naturalism.

George Burman Foster combined intellectual fearlessness with a never-shaken devotion to human values. The successive generations of students who passed through his classroom knew each a different thinker but the same great soul. His mind was constantly moving through the years so that it has become difficult for students of the earlier era to appreciate how radically different intellectually was the Foster of the later days. Yet the key to the transition is clear. It lies in his humanism. The stress on human values held him temporarily in the fold of Ritschlianism with its deep loyalty to Jesus. When that resting place was shaken he could not be satisfied with any form of modernism which saved theology in terms of metaphysical abstractions. His interest was not in the ideology of the past but in the vital issues of the moving process of social living. He welcomed the functional interpretation of religion and of theology which five years earlier he had denounced as a way of reducing God and religion to illusions. At last he could say: "Little by little, the man-agency takes the place of the god-agency; and corresponding to this man no longer finds that he now needs certainty, but uncertainty, the chance to venture and explore." "Must we know that values last forever before we will create them? A value is good while it lasts. Life is good even though it may not last forever." "Any alleged superhuman reality is an empty abstraction." Thus at the end he reached a naturalism rich with emotional qualities because inclusive of all the values of human creative attainment and possibility.

The last words of the last lecture given on the quadrangles before his death may well still stand as an appeal to religious men: "If religion, without science, fails and falls back by reversion to type to the form of superstition, science, without religion, would seem to be an engine for the destruction of the human race."

Friedrich Nietzsche needs no defender in our age, yet among the many works which attempt to interpret him, this work, done at a time when he lacked sympathetic spokesmen among the elect, should find its place and welcome. To the thousands of students of a great teacher it will bring memories of precious hours of inspiration.

A. EUSTACE HAYDON.

The University of Chicago

CONTENTS

FRIEDRICH NIETZSCHE

FRIEDRICH NIETZSCHE

CHAPTER ONE

THE LIFE AND WRITINGS OF FRIEDRICH NIETZSCHE

A PRELIMINARY word touching the name "Nietzsche" may be of interest to the reader. There is an adjective in the Czech language which means "humble" and is spelled *"nizky."* *"Nizky"* is frequently found as a name of many people in Germany having Slavic forefathers; the name acclimatized appears under various forms, such as *Nitzky, Nitzschke, Nietzsche,* all of which can be found in directories, according to Mügge, to whom I am indebted for this philological item.

Friedrich Nietzsche cherished a tradition that his ancestors were Polish, the Counts of Nietzki, who fled under persecution from Poland as religious refugees. So at least the boy was told, and he believed it gladly. This tradition had much to do in shaping the character of our proud, aristocratic thinker. He said one day: "A Count Nietzki must not lie." To be sure, no one has proved that Nietzsche's cherished belief is supported by facts. We do not know; even his sister uses the phrase, "somewhat mythical Polish descent,"—the only doubt she ever expressed respecting her brother's belief. I refer to this matter in order to point out the curious fact that Nietzsche, the champion of aristocratic radicalism, fierce opponent of current democracy, apostle of everything directed against humility, bore a name which literally means, "the humble man."

Nietzsche was born on October 15, 1844, in Röcken. His father, Karl Ludwig Nietzsche, was the pastor of this small solitary village situated in the Prussian province of Saxony. His father was the son and grandson of ecclesiastics, and his mother, Franziska Oehler, was the daughter and granddaughter of parsons. It is even said that Nietzsche came from seven generations of clergymen. A second curious fact is that Nietzsche, the apostle of Antichrist, was born in a German parsonage, and descended from parsons. His family was very religious, but I do not doubt that his subsequent violent antipathy to the established religion was due to an overplus of "official" piety in his youth.

When Nietzsche was four years old his father had a fall down a flight of steps, which resulted in a concussion of the brain. Thereafter, he suffered intermittently from the loss of reason. This fact has seemed to some critics to justify them in attempting to trace Nietzsche's final malady to hereditary predisposition—an absurd idea, for the boy came of good stock. His father lingered for a year and then mercifully died. This sad event made a profound impression on the boy Friedrich, who often referred to it in his later years.

There were two other children, a boy that lived but two years, and a girl, Elizabeth, who has been an eager chronicler of her famous brother's life and a rather too enthusiastic apologist of his philosophy.

After the death of his father, Nietzsche's mother moved in 1850 to Naumburg, a neighboring town, provincial, medieval, and conventional, run by a clique of lawyers, officials, parsons and old fogies. Nevertheless, the boy appears to have liked the somber town, and cherished the idea of becoming a parson himself; his schoolmates even nicknamed him "the parson." Although Nietzsche had some playmates, his permanent companions were women. He was brought up by women only, his mother, sister, grandmother, and two aunts composing the household. Of course, these feminine surroundings could not fail to exercise a definite influence upon him. Among their life-long results are to be recognized Nietzsche's great sensitiveness, his fondness for introspection, and perhaps his ardent love of poetry and music. And yet, as a third curious fact, he who was thus brought up, by and with women, became a confirmed antifeminist.

The boy was precocious, conscientious, earnest, and proud. On being sent to the grammar school, he felt so ill at ease that his mother transferred him to a private institution instead. Afterwards he entered Pforta, a boarding school, at the age of fourteen. The curriculum was classical, the discipline very rigid. This school gave Germany many great men, *e.g.*, Novalis, a poet and dreamer of lovely dreams (the German Maeterlinck); Schlegel, philologist and brilliant Shakespearean scholar; and Fichte, the great philosopher and patriot (the German John the Baptist).

Even before entering Pforta, Nietzsche, as we have seen, had acquired certain characteristics, which remained with him through life, his fondness for the "good form" that characterizes the best society, and his love of solitude, of poetry, of music. As early as 1854 (when but ten years old) he composed a motet in honor of his grandmother, and his first poetry dates back to this time.

Having lived under the softening home influence of women, he was not at first happy at Pforta. The routine and discipline were irksome, the hours long, the work hard, and there was not much real sport. To produce great scholars was the one aim of the school. Amid the daily monotony Nietzsche found some consolation in writing down what he saw, felt, and hoped. He kept a kind of diary—interesting, youthful jottings these—showing the lad's tendency to self-examination and self-consolation, sometimes premature when the boy of fourteen discusses the "three stages" of his poetical works; and even morbid when on his birthday he sees time passing like the rose of spring. The really important portions of the diary, however, are those which show how the young thinker gradually lost the belief of his fathers. He did not break away suddenly, but the writings of his favorite authors, Schiller, Hölderlin, especially Byron, together with the Higher Criticism of the Bible (Steinhart explains the Forty-fifth Psalm as an earthly marriage song) did not fail to move and dispose the young mind. Slowly he hauled up the anchors of his life's ship to leave the moorings of the authoritative creed of two thousand years' standing, and sailed forth without guide or compass upon the Ocean of Doubt.

We next find Nietzsche at the University of Bonn in 1864, at the age of twenty, with his friend Paul Deussen. He entered as a student of philology and theology, but discontinued theology with the close of his first semester.

We must bear in mind that the students in a German university lead, on the whole, a very independent and gay life, the memory of which never dies, and often sheds a soothing light over the evening of old age. At first the boisterous and rollicking habits of his jolly fellow students attracted Nietzsche. He became—for a time—one of the beer-drinking, singing, and dueling crowd. But the schoolmaster and the parson were still powerful in him. Soon he began to hate the drinking bouts in the evening, the dawdling and flirting in the streets, and withdrew more and more to his studies and his favorite recreation, music. Nietzsche's fellow students now nicknamed him "Sir Gluck" on account of his musical leanings. He often had to conduct musical affairs in his club, the Franconia. The great musical festivals in the neighboring Cologne were days of ecstasy to him.

At the University Nietzsche more and more turned away from the Christian beliefs, and one can imagine the horror of the respectable Mrs. Nietzsche when, during the Easter holiday of 1865, her son refused to go, as they were accustomed to do, to the Lord's Table. Later he wrote his sister Elizabeth, who was worrying about him, these remarkable words: "If you desire peace of soul and happiness, believe! If you want to be a disciple of truth, search!"

Meantime, in 1865 his favorite professor, Ritschl—Ritschl, without whom the sudden meteorlike official career of Nietzsche would never have been possible—went to Leipzig University, Nietzsche following him there. It was at Leipzig that Nietzsche happened one day to purchase in an antiquarian shop a copy of Schopenhauer's greatest book, *Die Welt als Wille und Vorstellung*. He was fascinated by the grim sage. This book revolutionized his outlook upon life, and completed his separation from Christianity. Subsequently he broke with his master, but never again escaped his influence, for traces of Schopenhauer's doctrines can be found in all the books that Nietzsche has written.

A word should be written in this connection about Nietzsche's military service. He was very short-sighted and even at Pforta had had trouble with his eyes; still in 1867 he had to go through one year's military service, against his expectations and wishes. But at that time the Prussian army needed more recruits, and the authorities enrolled men who were usually exempted. Young Nietzsche made the best of a bad job. He became a rather capable soldier, indeed, the best rider in his detachment. Did this help him toward a fondness for war and aristocracy? Or did he really have such a fondness? At any rate, after serving a few months and while mounting his horse, he lacerated some pectoral muscles. An operation became necessary, and no more active service was required of him.

The youth returned to his studies, to his beloved Professor Ritschl, to whom his brilliancy and thoroughness as a student had endeared him, and to his Greek philology and antiquity. Besides his response to Ritschl and Greek antiquity, two other influences in those Leipzig years were responsible for forming Nietzsche's personality. Reference has already been made to Schopenhauer. The other influence was Wagner.

Nietzsche was fond of music throughout his life. At this time he became acquainted with Wagner's music, and shortly afterwards with the master himself. The powerful personality of the great composer completely enchanted the young enthusiast, and made him a most fervent admirer and follower. Here we have another curious fact: Nietzsche, the independent one, became for a time the disciple of two masters. At this juncture a great surprise awaited him. In 1869, before he had taken his doctor's degree, and in spite of his youth—he was not yet twenty-five years old—the authorities of the Swiss University at Bâle, upon Ritschl's recommendation, appointed Nietzsche professor of classical philology. Ritschl wrote the Senate: "Nietzsche will be able to do anything he wants."

On May 28, 1869, Professor Friedrich Nietzsche delivered his inaugural lecture, entitled "Homer and Classical Philology." His initial salary was about six hundred dollars, raised a little after a year. That was not much, but he inherited some money from his Aunt Rosalie and from his uncle, who had made a fortune in England.

The people of Bâle are of a reserved character, and Nietzsche was lonely. But in August, 1869, he wrote a friend this letter:

I have found a man who personifies to me, as no one else does, that which Schopenhauer calls the "Genius," and who is entirely pervaded with that wonderful, heart-stirring philosophy. Such an absolute idealism prevails in him, such a deep and stirring humanism, such a lofty seriousness of life, that in his neighborhood I feel as near something divine.

This was in 1869. In 1888, Nietzsche called Wagner a "clever rattlesnake, a typical decadent"! What had happened? That is an epoch-making matter in Nietzsche's life, of which more will be said in a succeeding chapter.

Shortly afterwards, the Franco-Prussian war broke out, in July, 1870. Nietzsche took part as a volunteer nurse, his connection with a Swiss university requiring him to become a Swiss citizen, and forbidding his enlistment as a combatant. Unfortunately, he shortly became seriously ill, was incapacitated for further service, and so returned to his duties in Bâle. His war career was ended. Moreover, the impression of the horrors he had seen had been almost too much for him, and he never could be induced to talk of his experiences.

A fifth curious fact emerges: Nietzsche, who came to be the archenemy of narrow national ideals, asked his authorities for leave to go to the front as a nurse, in the cause of the Fatherland.

He returned, then, to Bâle and resumed his duties. But not for long. He had to pay the penalty of his daring campaign as nurse and of insufficient attention to his ailments, dysentery and diphtheria. He fell ill from violent neuralgia, insomnia, eye trouble, and indigestion. Two months' rest at Lugano, however, was sufficient to restore him to health.

Meantime his first book, *The Birth of Tragedy Out of the Spirit of Music*, was nearing completion; in 1871 it appeared in print at his own expense, as did all his books. It was an homage paid to Wagner. The keynote of the book is in these sentences: "Existence and the World appear justified only as an aesthetic phenomenon," and "Art supplies man with the necessary veil of illusion which is required for action; for the true knowledge as to the awfulness and absurdity of existence kills action."

Nietzsche here opposes the Greek culture existing before and after Socrates. The former civilization was intoxicated with its myths, its Dionysian songs; it was strong, cruel, grand. The latter was impious, rationalistic, bloodless, feeble. Nietzsche goes on to say that the culture of his day is on the whole too much like that of the past

Socratic period, but that salvation will come if the bidding of Wagner's great mystic music is followed.

The book was warmly received by a small circle of friends, especially by Wagnerians, and most especially by Wagner himself and his wife. But of course it met with a very chilling reception on the part of philologists generally. One of them, a fellow professor, called the book "pure nonsense." The general public ignored the book, and no capable reviewer took it up. One philologist went so far as to write a vitriolic and abusive pamphlet against it, but a friend, Rohde, published a brilliant counter-attack to that pamphlet. Yet Nietzsche was depressed. For a time he was professionally tabooed, and students were advised not to go to Bâle to study philology.

Another cause of sadness was added. Wagner left Tribschen, where Nietzsche had so often gone, for Bayreuth, where the great national opera house was being erected. Yet Nietzsche's old philological reputation was still great enough to bring some sunshine with these days. The Universities of Griefswald and of Dorpat each wanted the young professor. (We must assume that the book had not reached the authorities.) Nietzsche refused both offers, and the Bâle Senate raised his salary from six hundred dollars to eight hundred dollars, in recognition of his loyalty.

And now we are in the midst of things! From 1873 to 1876 in quick succession Nietzsche published four long essays: *David Strauss, Confessor and Writer; The Use and Abuse of History; Schopenhauer as Educator;* and *Richard Wagner in Bayreuth.* To Nietzsche, Strauss was a shallow, free-thinking optimist. His second book was an attack on the contemporaries and professors who made an idol out of historical learning. In the third book, Schopenhauer is the philosophical type of future man; state-paid university professors of philosophy are servile. The fourth book is a eulogy on Wagner. Nietzsche called the four books *Thoughts out of Season,* meaning that they excoriated faults and defects of his age.

These books are bitter, and Nietzsche's enemies grew. Worst of all, came the breach with Wagner. Nietzsche's first period was ended.

In his second period Nietzsche came to himself; more and more found his own way, his own philosophy, his own self. Schopenhauer and Wagner were discarded. A great change now came over him. From an enthusiastic Dionysian dreamer he turned into a calm Apollonian thinker. He began to distrust art and metaphysics, and to place his faith in science and research. The scholar prevailed over the artist, and he wrote *Human, all-too-Human,* a book for free spirits, 1878-1880—*The Monument of a Crisis*—as he calls it, *The Dawn of Day,* 1881; and *Joyful Wisdom,* 1882.

Shortly after Christmas, 1875, Nietzsche's health broke down, but he recovered during a vacation. In April, 1875, he fell in love with a charming Dutch lady, who refused to marry him because she said she was engaged to another. It took Nietzsche some time to rally from that, but he did so, and wrote like a demon. Then his health grew worse, and necessitated a year's vacation. He now met Rée, who became a friend and influenced Nietzsche toward determinism by drawing his attention to the English school of philosophy. Rée and Nietzsche went to Naples, and spent much time there in the company of Fräulein von Meysenbug, a society lady and authoress.

The three seem to have had a happy time together for over six months. Then, after a cure at a watering place, Nietzsche went back to Bâle and resumed his professorial duties.

Especially he wrote. Aphorism became his favorite vehicle of thought, probably owing to his poor health. Most of his thoughts occurred to him during his long and solitary walks, when he jotted down a few notes, which he polished later. Nietzsche was fond of comparing aphorisms with mountain peaks, and of declaring that in the mountains the shortest way is from peak to peak, but that for such a route one must have "long legs and be big and tall."

But Nietzsche's eyes, stomach, and head were the demons that would never let him alone. His health grew worse and worse until it finally broke down completely, and in 1879 he resigned his professorship. The Senate thanked him for his services and granted a pension of six hundred dollars.

He went to Sils-Maria in the Ober-Engadine, recovered a little, and wrote. Then he grew worse; his sufferings were almost unbearable, and he thought that death was near. But he lived through his pain, and spent the spring at Venice, a city which had a most beneficial effect upon him.

Henceforth, Nietzsche was a solitary, restless wanderer, now in Italy, now the Engadine, now Germany, drifting from place to place, searching for health and friends, or for solitude and truth. He led a most frugal life, often preparing his simple meals himself on a spirit lamp. Sometimes in the evenings headaches would torment him and without lighting up he would stretch himself out on the sofa. "He is too poor to burn candles," said his neighbors, so they often offered him some. He thanked them, and explained, but they called him *Il Santo,* The Saint. He spent the mornings in long solitary walks along the sea coasts or in the mountains; always thinking and dreaming, his notebook his only constant companion.

As I have indicated, *Human, all-too-Human* was a transitional work. But *Dawn of Day* suggests the dawn of his own, his very own, philosophy. Nietzsche thinks now that it is only from the sciences of physiology and medicine that we can borrow the foundation stones of new ideals. He tries hard to look at nature without juggling into it finality or a purpose.

At this time, on the majestic and rocky heights of Sils-Maria, the exciting thought of the Eternal Recurrence occurred to him. Afterwards, the influence of this sad metaphysical idea began to depress him. Once more, however, the sun broke through, and in 1882 he wrote his brightest book, *Joyful Wisdom,* an aphorism book, vigorous, pulsing, life-loving. The disheartening idea of the Eternal Recurrence is now displaced by the more stimulating vision of the Superman, and Zarathustra is mentioned for the first time.

In 1882, Nietzsche traveled in the spring to Sicily. There he accepted an invitation from Fräulein von Meysenbug to come to Rome. She adored Nietzsche's personality and genius. She wanted to find him a wife, especially since he wrote her: "I tell you in confidence, what I need is a good woman." She selected Fräulein Lou Salomé, twenty years of age. Nietzsche promptly fell in love with her, proposed, and was rejected. Things happened behind the scenes here; what, it is hard to say, since the only two surviving actors, the Fräulein and the sister, say hard things about each other. I suppose it was just a human episode, in which Nietzsche lost a potential wife and his friend Rée, whom he thought guilty of treachery in the affair.

More lonely than ever, Nietzsche set out again upon his wanderings. But his love now concentrated on his spiritual child, *Zarathustra,* the finest artistic creed in modern literature. The blind, hopeless medievalism of the Eternal Recurrence no longer satisfied him. He wanted to pass the human goal, to eulogize action, to ennoble man through the ideal of the Superman.

I teach you the Superman. Man is something that is to be surpassed. What have you done to surpass man? All beings hitherto have created something beyond themselves, and ye want to be the ebb of that great tide, and would rather go back to the beast than surpass man? . . . The Superman is the meaning of the earth. Let your *will* say: The Superman *shall be* the meaning of the earth! I conjure you, my brethren, *remain true to the earth;* and believe not those who speak unto you of superearthly hopes!

With that joyous note does the book open; with this gospel Zarathustra comes down from his mountain.

The book was written during 1883 and 1884. It did not appeal to Nietzsche's contemporaries, and had no sale. The fourth part was printed privately at Nietzsche's expense, forty copies to be distributed among his friends. But he was so lonely that he could muster only seven people to whom he might send copies. Practically no reviewer, no critic, took any notice of the book that

Nietzsche later called the deepest book and the greatest gift that has ever been bestowed upon mankind.

In 1886, came his next book, *Beyond Good and Evil;* and in 1887, *The Genealogy of Morals.* Under what conditions did man invent for himself those judgments of values, Good and Evil? What is the basis of the justification involving good and evil? If life is worth living, what is it that makes it so? Is there an authority higher than myself? If self-sacrifice were consistently adhered to, would it not result in a personality that ought to be sacrificed, the sooner the better? Can we give up pity and keep love? These are great questions.

In October, 1887, we find Nietzsche at Nice. Here he lost one of his oldest and best friends through misunderstanding; but here at last he found two distinguished readers, the famous Dane, George Brandes; and the French historian, Taine, who encouraged and applauded him. In April, 1888, George Brandes wrote him that he was going to deliver a course of lectures on Nietzsche's philosophy, an utterance that fell like a ray of hope across the latter's dreary life.

Nietzsche's last books are: *Will to Power,* a transvaluation of values; *The Case of Wagner,* written within May and June, 1886; *The Twilight of the Idols,* written in feverish haste in a few days; and *Antichrist.* One more book came from his pen, a kind of autobiography, *Ecce Homo,* a fitting coping stone to his work before his mental death in January, 1889.

During the last months of 1888, spent in Turin, Nietzsche was in a happy, bright mood. George Brandes had procured him another reader, the Swede, August Strindberg. Taine in Paris; Strindberg in Sweden; Brandes

[14]

in Denmark—the dawn of Nietzsche's fame! But it was too late, and Nietzsche seems to have known it.

What was the cause of Nietzsche's insanity? "An exogenous disease," said Mobius; but Dr. Gould, a medical man, replies that the assertion is contradicted by every fact of Nietzsche's life, character, and illness. And Professor Kaftan, who knew Nietzsche well, writes: "I can but say that I have never heard of any such excesses on the part of Nietzsche, and from my personal acquaintance with the man I demand that they must be entirely ruled out." "War experiences, chloral, and an unknown drug," says his sister. "Inherited disposition to neurotic disorder," says Paul Carus. "Overwork, worry, disappointment, loneliness, plus his sister's view," says Mügge. What caused Nietzsche's insanity? We do not know.

Perhaps Nietzsche could say, as Byron said, in *Childe Harold's Pilgrimage:*

> . . . I have thought
> Too long and darkly, till my brain became,
> In its own eddy boiling and o'erwrought,
> A whirling gulf of phantasy and flame.

CHAPTER TWO

Nietzsche and Schopenhauer

WHEN he was twenty-one, and living in Leipzig, Nietzsche happened one day to purchase in an antiquarian's shop (in fact, in the shop of Rohn, the bookseller, with whom he was lodging), a copy of Schopenhauer's *Die Welt als Wille und Vorstellung*. A single reading sufficed. Schopenhauer had made a new convert, one who, although he subsequently broke with his master, never again escaped his influence. At the first perusal he was overwhelmed by the magnificent prospects opened out to him by this book and even more so by the personality of the philosopher himself, whom he perceived behind the book. In Nietzsche's *Schopenhauer as Educator* (Section 2) the following confession occurs:

> I am one of those readers of Schopenhauer who know for certain, after they have read a page of him, that they will read this book from the first to the last, and that they will listen with rapt attention to every word that falls from his lips. My confidence in him was instantly full and entire.

In 1874, Nietzsche wrote again in this appreciative way:

> Schopenhauer's speeches are to himself alone, or, if you wish to imagine an auditor, let it be a son whom the father is instructing. It is a rough, honest, good-humored talk to one who "hears and loves." Such writers are rare. His strength

and sanity surround us at the first sound of his voice; it is like entering the heights of the forest where all breathe deep and are well again. We feel a bracing air everywhere, a certain candor and naturalness of his own, that belong to men who are at home with themselves and master of a very rich home indeed.

For once, then, Nietzsche was grateful, grateful to a man, a thinker, who initiated him into the life of the spirit, and taught him to see reality as it is, with all its ugliness, and with all the sufferings it brings with it.

Late in 1865, Nietzsche's letters were full of Schopenhauerian pessimism. He even sought to convert his womenfolk to the doctrine, as the following letter may serve to indicate:

. . . Dear friends, There are two roads: either we accustom ourselves to be as narrow as may be, and to turn the light of our wits as low as possible, and then seek riches and to live on the pleasures of the world; or, we know that . . . we are the slaves of life the more we enjoy it, and so we discard the goods of this world, practice abstinence, are mean toward ourselves and loving to all others—simply because we pity our comrades in misery—in short, we live according to the strict precepts of primitive Christianity, not of the modern sugary and formless Christianity.

Such was the beginning, and in this temper of mind he wrote the books of his first, or artistic period, namely; *The Birth of Tragedy* (1871), *Thoughts out of Season* (1872-1873), and especially *Schopenhauer as Educator* (1873-1876).

But very soon, in the second,—positivistic, intellectualistic, or scientific—period, Nietzsche had resigned his place in the school of Schopenhauer, and was writing

Human, all-too-Human in its various parts, especially *The Wanderer and his Shadow* (1876-1879) and *The Dawn of Day* (1880-1881). In these books we find him rejecting the ideal of the artist and accepting the life-ideal of the scientist. It is not the artistic man through his subjective consructions who enfranchises us, it is the scientific man through his objective thought who is free himself, and who makes us free. But in rejecting the artistic ideal of life, Nietzsche rejected with it its presupposition, namely, the Schopenhauerian metaphysics, along with its pessimism and nihilism. He became a sober empiricist. It is no longer Schopenhauer and Wagner, representatives of art; it is Socrates and Voltaire, representatives of intellectualism.

Then ensues Nietzsche's third period, in which he turns away from intellectualism back to Schopenhauer's voluntarism, from which he set out. But when he went back to Schopenhauer, he took with him the optimism of his second period. Henceforth, he is not a pessimistic but an optimistic Schnopenhauer, *mutatis mutandis!*

The books of this third period are *The Joyful Wisdom* (1882); *Thus Spake Zarathustra* (1883-1885); *Beyond Good and Evil* (1885-1886); *The Genealogy of Morals* (1887); *The Twilight of the Idols* (1888); and *The Antichrist* (1888). Nietzsche now accepts substantially, but with changes to be discussed later, Schopenhauer's doctrine of the will, rejecting pessimism violently. Indeed, in *Zarathustra* he cannot say too hard things about "world-contemners," "world-deniers," "men faithless to earth, of whom the earth is weary; so away with them!" "There was a time," he exclaims, "when the greatest sin was blasphemy against God . . . the greatest sin now is blasphemy against the earth." "People meet an invalid, or an old man, or a corpse—and immediately they say: 'Life is refuted!' But they only are refuted, and their eye, which seeth only one side of existence." "I tell you there are higher problems than the pleasure-pain problems." Again, "The discipline of suffering, of great suffering; know you not that it is only this discipline that has produced all the elevations of humanity hitherto?" In a word, the great question according to Nietzsche is this: Which of the valuing codes do you mean to adopt as the highest? According to what criterion do you approve or disapprove of the world? Pleasure, beauty, virtue,—what is your standard of judgment? Nietzsche accepts Schopenhauer's judgment of what the world is—godless, chaotic, meaningless, goalless—accepts Schopenhauer's premise, but denies his conclusion, pessimism, and affirms optimism. To be sure it is an unusual kind of optimism, denied to be such by not a few; but optimism it is, for all that.

Now that the great and beautiful problem has been roughly stated, we must try to penetrate a little into the heart of the matter. But first, who was this Schopenhauer, and was there some spiritual affinity between him and Friedrich Nietzsche?

I can hardly undertake here to tell the story of his life (1788-1860) but can at least characterize him. One might sum it up by saying that Schopenhauer lived a self-indulgent life, and wrote sentimentally about Nirvana, while Nietzsche lived an ascetic, austere life of consummate saintliness and wrote in sunny joyousness the glad gospel of the Superman. One might say that; but, to be entirely fair, one must say a little more than that.

Schopenhauer was the son of a wealthy merchant; his

mother was a brilliant novelist; he himself was a master in both literary style and philosophic system-making. Jean Paul's famous characterization of Schopenhauer's *Die Welt als Wille und Vorstellung* is to the point: "A book of philosophic genius, bold, many-sided, full of skill and depth, but of a depth often hopeless and bottomless, akin to that melancholy lake in Norway in whose deep waters, beneath the steep rock walls, one never sees the sun, but only the stars reflected, and no bird or wave ever flies over its surface." It is precisely this calm of Schopenhauer's intellect that is the characteristic thing about his writings; and no one who knows the highly intellectual and reflective type of the nervously burdened genius will fail to comprehend the meaning of the contrast between the man's peevishness, which tortured him, and his thinking, wherein he found rest. He embodied a profound contrast between the contemplative and the passionate life.

Schopenhauer was hereditarily burdened in respect of nerves. His pessimism must, therefore, be associated with his temperament. He had neurasthenic symptoms, such as night terrors, causeless depressions, a persistent dread of possible misfortunes, a complaining and frequently unbearable ill-humor, crises of violent temper, and yet a fine general constitution. As I say, this gives rise to the question whether Schopenhauer's pessimism was mainly due to mere morbidness of temperament—*stimmung pessimismus,* as the Germans say. As a fact, he was incapable of a permanently cheerful view of life, a born outcast, doomed to hide and be lonely. As a fact, he was given to pettiness in the minor relations of life, was vain, uncompanionable, and bitter.

But then, many clever men have had all those burdens to bear, without being able to see the tragedy of life as wisely and deeply as Schopenhauer saw it. It will not do, in any event, to state the case against his pessimism in such shallow fashion as to make it appear that, while all pessimism is mere pettiness, all optimism is *prima facie* noble-mindedness. Optimism also can be selfish and even intolerable. For myself, I am disposed to say, as a matter of mere historical judgment, this: Schopenhauer's nervous burdens unquestionably opened his eyes to the particular aspect of life which he found so tragic, but the fact of such burdens is of no service to us in forming our estimate of the ultimate significance of his philosophic insight —an insight which, for my part, I find as deep as it was partial. But what now was that insight? What was the gist of his philosophic view of the world and his judgment of life?

Schopenhauer's philosophical views, as the title of his main work, *Die Welt als Wille und Vorstellung,* indicates, may be divided into two separate groups, *Idea* and *Will.* He starts out as an extreme idealist. The world is only *idea* of the subject; self-knowledge is directed solely to the phenomena or appearance of things. The *matter,* the substance, which somehow gives occasion for these appearances, is inaccessible. The world as *idea,* therefore, is a construction of our thought. We analyze the mass of ideas into groups; we give them laws; we consider them as if they were real, but in fact there is no bridge from idea to thing. Rather, Schopenhauer dares to place the idea-world on the same plane with our dream experiences. We have here, then, an apprehension of the unreality of human ideation, a conception that is oppressive

[21]

to the human spirit. Schopenhauer saw that it was desirable to set over against this idealism another activity of the human spirit. This different activity puts another kind of construction upon the world, another meaning in it. He now bases his metaphysics on the knowledge of his own nature as *will,* a knowledge immediately given to man. Man's own bodily life is given to man, not simply as idea, but as real to him in the activity of his will. Every act of will is a movement of the body, and every movement of this body is an act of will. In this alone is there reality. Body in the will becomes visible. Schopenhauer now turns to the larger body, the cosmos, to interpret it according to his view of will-body, body-will. As every sensible or spiritual relation of man is referred to his simple, essential kernel, the will, so the will is conceived as manifesting itself in all natural phenomena, emerging there, gaining self-dependence there. The externalization of will begins down in inorganic nature—begins without consciousness, blindly, out of mere causation. In the vegetative life, will phenomenalizes through mere stimulation; in animal life through motivation also. It is only through the motivation of perception that the animal is brought to an expression of will. But man is brought to an expression of will through logical, conceptual, abstract motive also. While the manifestation of will is thus diverse— and there is a principle of individuation—yet the will itself is unitary from its lowest to its highest stage: *it is the will to live, to life, in indivisible, unceasing, unresting motion.*

Thus, briefly, compactly, proceeds Schopenhauer's metaphysic of nature. On this foundation he builds his æsthetics and his ethics. His æsthetics has a wholly contemplative character, is entirely will-less, and elevates us above the driving and the doing of tyrannical will into the beatific blessedness of vision. *Extinction of individuality and of will is the supreme goal of æsthetic gratification.*

The ethics of Schopenhauer takes on a religious hue in its approximation to the Buddhistic thought of redemption. It belongs to the nature of will ever to affirm life. It is on this account that he arrives at his pessimistic conception of the *perniciousness and detestableness of this will.* So his ethics urges the negation of this will which affirms life. As cardinal virtues which are hostile to will and to life, he names righteousness and human love, both reposing on *pity,* a feeling that is thoroughly hostile to life. Asceticism is a great aid in turning away from will— an alienation, estrangement from will. Death consummates such an aversion from will—death, which as negation of life brings the longed-for redemption from the restless will. So, his line of thought consistently ends in the Buddhistic requirement of the negation of life, which is clothed in the garment of religious redemption, as supreme and final serenity and satisfaction.

Such, in outline, is a fair statement of the egoistic and pessimistic philosophy of Arthur Schopenhauer. It was reënforced and made attractive through the literary skill of its author,—Schopenhauer, Nietzsche and Bismarck writing the finest German of modern times. It was reënforced also by the masterly fashion in which he harmonized it with the natural science of his day. His appeal to the mystic side of reality, moreover, supplemented gratefully the cold, objective, scientific processes. His doctrine of redemption, so different from church redemption, appealed to many idealistic souls, who, in spite of materialistic science, hungered for some release from the weary weight of the unintelligible world. Schopenhauer's views still persist, not so much through his own works, not now extensively read, but rather through the influence of Nietzsche, and especially through the art of Richard Wagner, whose operas have astonishingly spread the pessimistic world view and redemption doctrine, together with the genuinely Schopenhauerian, purely physiological conception of the relation between man and woman. Von Hartmann continued and extended Schopenhauer's views.

The exclusion of all historical interest on the part of Schopenhauer has avenged itself during the last decade in the person of his disciple, Arthur Drews, resulting in an even greater misunderstanding of the Christian religion of the First Century. German philosophy to-day holds that the overcoming of the bad after-effects of Schopenhauer's genius is one of the tasks of the German philosophic future. Still, under the lead of Professor Paul Deussen, a Schopenhauer Society has been formed, which does not indicate that his influence has waned.

After this all-too summary exposition, we may return to Friedrich Nietzsche, for we are now in a position to permit the following statement of his basic principle, from which consistently all the various streams of his thought issue.

The real kernel of Nietzsche, then, in my opinion, is this: Nietzsche's doctrine is Schopenhauerism given a positive instead of a negative turn of application. This alteration, or, if the reader will, revaluation, took place under the influence of Charles Darwin. Nietzscheanism is equal to Schopenhauerism plus Darwinism, each of the two modified by the other, and both transmuted in the alembic of Nietzsche's own original genius. At all events, this is my thesis, which I wish to verify in subsequent chapters by referring thereto for explanation all the main movements of Nietzsche's thought.

As I have already pointed out, Nietzsche passed through several periods of development before he reached his own original doctrine. In the first period, as I have said, Nietzsche was mainly a Schopenhauerean. *The Birth of Tragedy, Thoughts out of Season,* and especially *Schopenhauer as Educator* prove this assertion. His Schopenhauerism was colored, to be sure, by Richard Wagner, with whom we shall deal later. The main features of Schopenhauer's philosophy are to be found in Schopenhauer's metaphysics of the will and in his pessimism. For Nietzsche, too, the world is will and idea! For Nietzsche, too, the insatiable and eternally unsatisfied will is the foundation of all our misery and torment. Moreover, Nietzsche, also, finds redemption from this torment of will in æsthetic idea and production, therefore in art, so that the artist is ideal for Nietzsche. This artist-ideal he sees realized in Richard Wagner; this art-ideal he sees realized in Wagner's dramatic music. The artist, through his art, frees himself and his brothers from the torment and torture of the will and of illusion. It was in this sense that Wagner named his house at Bayreuth—*Wahnfried.*

Now, the presupposition of this art enthusiasm is pessimism—pessimism which sees in the usual living and dying of men, only ever-new forms of blind, insatiable will and illusion. Art lifts man above himself and out of his pain, frees him from his self, makes him noble and good, and even holy. In this sense, art is the necessary complement of the tragic disposition, which Nietzsche, with Schopenhauer, required of men of deep thought and high endeavor, in opposition to the "incurable," "enervating" optimism of the type which, as represented in and by David Strauss, was anathematized by Nietzsche.

Even the Greeks, from whom art, and especially tragedy, were first born, were pessimists, at least the nobler Greeks, *e.g.,* Empedocles. The rationalist Socrates was an optimist, but with Socrates the decay of genuine Hellenism begins. But only the *tragic* man is the true teacher of man. Schopenhauer, therefore, was the best *educator* also. Only the tragic artist produces truly liberating art; Richard Wagner, therefore, is the best artist.

But Nietzsche was soon to experience a fearful disillusionment. He had come to know Wagner in Switzerland and was intoxicated with the Nibelungen. But at Bayreuth Wagner did not seem to be the same man. Apparently petty traits of vanity and envy, of egoism and caprice disturbed Wagner, the idealist, who was not in the habit of separating ideal and reality. These bad personal qualities destroyed the artist-ideal. And when *Parsifal* came to light, the ideal of the Wagnerian art was destroyed for Nietzsche; for, in *Parsifal,* Nietzsche saw an unworthy genuflexion of his former sovereign artist before the altar,—a humiliation, a debasement of art through church. Nietzsche was horrified at this turn of the Wagnerian course of life. Nietzsche was a worshiper of classic antiquity. He was a classic philologist from conviction. He belonged to the generation of the Renaissance, humanists who could not forgive Christianity for causing the downfall of antique *kultur.* In his very first work, *The Birth of Tragedy,* he had tried to fuse the

German Nibelung music of Wagner with Greek art. But he now saw Wagner putting his wonderful art at the service of the medieval ideal in *Parsifal*. Here, then, the Nietzsche who was at home in classic antiquity, living in it and on it, proudly favoring it as a humanist in preference to Christianity and medievalism—this Nietzsche now experienced disillusion in the cruelest epoch of his life. With nausea, he turned his back upon his hitherto deified ideal, Richard Wagner. But to what did he turn? With characteristic one-sidedness and violence he now rushed into the science camp. Not art, but *science,* is ideal now. He substituted objectivity, for subjectivity, experience and exact observation for the metaphysics and pessimism and nihilism of Schopenhauer.

His slogan was: Only experience and its utilization through the understanding, excluding metaphysics on the one hand, and the unquiet, impulsive life on the other; only *empirical understanding!* Nietzsche, the passionate man, now found his satisfaction transitorily in science as in a kind of medical institution, a Karlsbad.

The Schopenhauerian metaphysics of the will was forsaken. Nietzsche was at this time a sober empiricist. He dedicated his books to the memory of Voltaire. In his first period he despised the rationalistic Socrates, who died without pathos, as Schopenhauer lived with nothing else. Now he adored Socrates—Socrates and Voltaire, *advocates of intellectualism, who saw in the victory of the intellect the victory of the good* and were, therefore, representatives of optimism. Nietzsche turned his back upon pessimism consistently with his new point of view. Pessimism passed consistently with the passing of the metaphysics of the will.

Furthermore, another change of great importance took place at this time. In his first period, under the influence of the unhistorical standpoint of Schopenhauer, he complained of the exaggeration of history in education and life. But in this second period, the historical treatment of things and their evolution became a problem of interest to him. In this connection Darwinism became for him a matter of profound study. Especially did he turn his attention to the development of moral ideas and to the problem of the progress of *kultur*.

Nietzsche's nature, however, was impulsive and passionate, and he could not tent long in his pathetic pilgrimage in the camp ground of the scientist. The golden mean was not for him. He must mount to the highest heights or descend to the deepest deeps. Science is objective, dispassionate, judicial, complacent. Not so Nietzsche, who was artist and prophet more than scientist. So, in his third period, he turned back to his old self again, but in a new form. From Schopenhauer's voluntarism he had set out on his pilgrimage; to it he now returned. As soldiers might wander over a trackless plain during the day, and return at night to the same camp fires which they had left in the morning, but return modified by the experience of their day's march, so Nietzsche returned to Schopenhauer, enriched and modified by the experiences of his second, the science period.

What was it that Nietzsche carried out of his second period into his third? Not only an interest in history, not only an interest in the historical development of morals and of *kultur* in general, but a particular optimism—the vital, joyous affirmation of the world and the will to live. He returned—this is the crucial and all-important point in the understanding of Nietzsche's philosophy—he returned to exactly Schopenhauer's world and Schopenhauer's will, that world of torture and of tears; but, whereas Schopenhauer cried *"Pessimism"* as he peered into the black abyss, Nietzsche shouted *"Optimism."* Schopenhauer with his splendid health and magnificent fortune, landed in pessimism; Nietzsche, "the crucified one," as he signed himself in his letters sometimes, in his nameless agony, landed in optimism, while facing the same Schopenhauerian facts. There is a psychological problem of the first rank.

In this third period, Nietzsche returns to Schopenhauer in so far as he accepts Schopenhauer's doctrine of the will of the world. But art no longer, as in the first period, seems to him to be the redeemer and liberator from the slavery to and torment of the blind will. Nietzsche took the optimism of the second period into the third; consequently, the will seemed to him no longer as blind, unhappy, needful of redemption, but as Will to Power, unbroken, fresh, glad of life, even though that life, like his own—not like Schopenhauer's—was one long crucifixion!

According to Nietzsche now, life is simply power and the practice of power. Life reposes on the instinct of the Will to Power, of the exercise of power; the will to life of Schopenhauer is now rebaptized as the Will to Power. To live is to widen out on all sides the sphere of power. This Will to Power is the instinctive basic impulse of all creatures. Naturally, however, these diverse Wills to Power must fall into conflict with each other. They reciprocally fight to the death with the powerful and irresistible instincts which spring out of the Will to

Power. It was just in this conflict of the different will-centers that Schopenhauer had discerned the evil in the world; evil toward whose delineation he could not do enough; evil from which Schopenhauer sought redemption in art, on the one hand, and in asceticism, on the other. What does Nietzsche see in the struggle of these diverse will-centers? Just the opposite—*the principle of the development of all Kultur*. Hence his hatred now of everything that would do away with that struggle, since it is the source of the elevation of the type man. Hence, I say, his hatred of morality, socialism, democracy, feminism, intellectualism, pessimism, Christianity, as he understood them. He hated with abysmal hatred all of these, because they softened, or eliminated, or neutralized that struggle among the will-centers which, in his belief, was the *sine qua non* of overcoming the decadence of his day and of insuring that life should travel once again the ascending curve of existence. Nietzsche could say: "I am come that ye may have power, and have it more abundantly"; Schopenhauer had to say: "I am come that ye may have weakness, and have it more despairingly." Great Nietzsche! We shall hardly see his like again. He has posed the question of fact for our generation and for all generations: Do the seven things I have enumerated—moralism, socialism, democracy, feminism, intellectualism, pessimism, Christianism—do these seven things weaken or strengthen the soul of man? That is the question of questions and the problem of problems; and it is the imperishable merit of Friedrich Nietzsche to have raised it squarely and fearlessly. Nietzsche was our modern Heraclitus: War is the father of all things; out of war and struggle arise all development. These seven foes of War are the foes of development.—"Down with them," therefore cries Nietzsche.

But there was another man who ascribed a similar, life-promoting effect to struggle: Charles Darwin. According to Darwin, the struggle for existence is the condition of all higher unfolding of organism. In the struggle for existence power increases, and the most powerful triumph. The weaker are driven to the wall and deserve to go down. Nature wills the victory to the stronger, and perfects species through that victory and the overthrow of the weaker. In dithyrambic swing, Nietzsche celebrates this natural law, whose pitilessness was to him something sublime and ennobling.

We have reached now the innermost kernel of Nietzsche's view of life, namely, the Schopenhauerian doctrine of will, given positive features under the influence of Darwin and his doctrine of the struggle of existence.

CHAPTER THREE

NIETZSCHE AND WAGNER

IN the previous chapter we have discussed the influence of Schopenhauer upon Nietzsche. We must now consider Wagner in similar relation. For Schopenhauer and Wagner, as we have seen, were the two early masters of Nietzsche, from whom he conquered his emancipation.

The Nietzsche and Wagner drama played itself out in three acts: the act of self-surrendering devotion; the act of temptation; and the act of victorious enfranchisement. I shall take these three periods of Nietzsche's experience in their order.

Nietzsche's admiration for Wagner goes back to the years of his youth. He was an uncompromising classicist until he reached the age of fifteen. This must have been due, in part, to the women who brought him up. He was an exclusive admirer of Mozart and Haydn, Schubert and Mendelssohn, Beethoven and Bach; and he was a decided scorner of what he called "the music of the future—of a Liszt or a Berlioz." So he began, but he finished by learning to enjoy the work of Wagner, and his admiration turned into enthusiasm when he heard *Tristan und Isolde*. "From the moment that *Tristan* was arranged for the piano I was a Wagnerite," he declares (1888), in speaking of the memories of his youth. The autumn holidays of 1862 were spent by him and a friend in playing this arrangement for the piano from morning till night. "Wonderfully beautiful!" he said to his sister. "Don't you think so?" "No," she replied. Their powerful voices often reminded her, she afterwards wrote, "of the howling of wolves." Such was the beginning of the Wagnerian experience of Nietzsche when he was a schoolboy at Pforta.

In 1868 Nietzsche was introduced to Wagner, when the master was staying with his relatives at Leipzig. Wagner's sister there was the wife of Professor Brockhaus. Nietzsche had already been hearing Wagner's music at concerts.

The reader will be interested in this letter written by Nietzsche to his friend Rohde, October, 1868:

This evening I was at the Euterpe Society, which has started its winter concerts, and I refreshed myself with the prelude to *Tristan und Isolde* as well as the overture to the *Meistersinger.* I cannot get myself to regard this music coldly and critically; every tissue and every nerve vibrate in me, and for a long time I have not had such an enduring feeling of rapture as when listening to the last-mentioned overture. My permanent seat as a subscriber is surrounded by critical spirits; immediately in front of me there sits Bernsdorff, the abomination I have spoken to you about; on my left Dr. Paul, the present hero of the *Tageblatt;* two places to the right of me is my friend Stede, who grinds out musical opinions for *Brendel's Musical Journal.* It is a thorny corner, and when we four all shake our heads together, it means disaster.

I must quote a scrap from another letter to Rohde:

I have one woman more particularly in view, of whom wonderful things have been told me; she is the wife of Professor Brockhaus and a sister of Richard Wagner's; and my

[33]

friend Windisch, who has just now called upon me, gave me a surprising account of her capacities. What pleased me about all this is that it confirms Schopenhauer's theory of heredity. Wagner's other sister, who was formerly an actress in Dresden, is also said to have been a very distinguished woman.

Then came Nietzsche's visit to the Brockhaus home. He describes his feelings to Rohde in still another letter, November 9, 1868:

When I reached home yesterday I found a card addressed to me with this note upon it: "Do you wish to make the acquaintance of Richard Wagner? If so, meet me at a quarter to four in the Theatre Café. Windisch." This news, I can assure you, so turned my head that I quite forgot what I was doing before it came, and was thoroughly bewildered.

To make a long story short, Wagner did not appear, as fate would have it, but in a few days Nietzsche did meet Wagner and wrote thus to Rohde:

Now let me give you a brief account of what happened that evening: really, the joys experienced were of such a rare and stimulating nature that even to-day I am not back in my old humdrum existence again, but can think of nothing better to do than to come to you, my dear friend, and tell you these wonderful tidings. Wagner played to us before and after supper, and got through every one of the more important passages of the *Meistersinger*. He imitated all the voices and was in very high spirits; he is, by the by, an extraordinarily active and fiery man. He speaks very quickly, shows considerable wit, and can make a private company of the sort assembled on that evening quite jolly. I managed to have a somewhat lengthy talk with him about Schopenhauer. Oh, you will understand what a joy it was for me to hear him speak with such indescribable warmth of our master,—what a lot he owed to him, how he was the only philosopher who had recognized the essence of music! Then he inquired as to how the professors were disposed toward him; laughed a good deal at the Philosophers' Congress at Prague, and spoke of the "philosophical journeymen." . . . At the close of the evening he . . . kindly asked me to visit him in order that we might have some music and philosophy together.

Thus began Nietzsche's personal acquaintance with Richard Wagner, the strongest influence that was ever exercised over him. For a decade since the publication of von Bülow's piano arrangement of *Tristan und Isolde* he had been a passionate admirer of Wagner's music, even though he had already rejected *Tannhäuser, Lohengrin,* and *Die Walküre.* But when Wagner, the man, came before him, with all the fascination of his strong will, Nietzsche felt at once that he was in the presence of a person who, in his volitional power, was of all his contemporaries most like himself. Nietzsche was the first person who, with one enthusiastic impulse, loved both Schopenhauer and Wagner, and the first of that band of young men, young Germany, who wrote the two names, Schopenhauer and Wagner, side by side, upon their banner.

Let me now attempt to unroll one of the most memorable dramas in the history of friendship and of genius, and later to disclose and examine the root of it all philosophically in character and in life.

In 1869 Nietzsche was a professor of philology at Bâle. During the years of his professorship there, from 1869 until 1876, he was on terms of the closest intimacy with Wagner and his wife, Frau Cosima. He frequently visited them in their retreat at Tribschen, and these visits remained the sweetest and most beautiful memories of Nietzsche's, and indeed of Wagner's career. The reader will find illuminating a fragment from another letter of Nietzsche to Baron von Gersdorff, August, 1869:

> In addition to this I have found a man who has revealed to me, as no other man could, the image of that which Schopenhauer calls "the genius," and who is thoroughly permeated by that wonderfully profound philosophy. This man is no other than Richard Wagner, about whom you need not take for granted any opinion which you may find in the press or the writings of musical experts, etc. *No one* can know him or judge him, because the whole world stands upon a basis different from his, and is not familiar with his atmosphere. He is ruled by such an absolute knowledge of ideality, by such profound and touching humanity, and by such a lofty and serious interest in life, that at his side I feel in the presence of the divine.

Halcyon, idyllic Tribschen days were these for Nietzsche and Wagner—days that were the great noontide of their friendship. Tribschen, beautifully situated at the foot of Mount Pilatus, was in itself an abode of happiness, a haven of refuge, the island of the blessed, to Nietzsche. Here his ideal of friendship seemed to become realized, and he believed in the elevating power of friendship. Perhaps these delightful days, when each of the two lonely, isolated and misunderstood men warmed his life at the other's hearthside suggested Nietzsche's poem on friendship:

> Hail, thou friendship
> Of my highest longing,
> Earliest red of morning!
> Endless often

Seemed the path, and night to me,
All things living
Hateful without aim!
Now will I live doubly,
When in thine eyes I have
Beheld victory and dawn:
Thou dearest Goddess!

By-the-by [he writes Erwin Rohde], I also have my Italy, just as you have; the one difference being that the only time I can keep for enjoying it consists of my Saturdays and Sundays. This Italy is called Tribschen, and I am already quite at home there.

Meanwhile Wagner was at work on the composition of *Siegfried,* and dreaming his big dream of Bayreuth, where the gigantic Nibelung drama in its unique style was to be elaborated to the German people, and later to all the world. Meanwhile, also, Nietzsche read the proof of Wagner's autobiography, meant only for a few friends, and entered into elevated conversation with the master. And meanwhile both were cherishing a common world-view, the Schopenhauerian doctrine of redemption, in which art plays so important a rôle. Wagner was, then, to Nietzsche, not only a fatherly friend, an adored artist, but the living embodiment of the philosophic spirit.

But the question arose (it was a way of Wagner's to see that it should arise): How could Nietzsche serve Wagner and Wagner's ambition? Nietzsche had already converted his friends Rohde and Gersdorff to Wagner's cause, as he had earlier won them over to Schopenhauer, but this conversion was more an outflow of friendly feeling than an act in the service of the Wagnerian mission. To work for Wagner, as he and no other could do, not as a noisy partisan propagandist, not as an unfree expounder of Wagner's opera, but as a new and powerful colleague, he had to employ his scholarship, his profound absorption in classic antiquity, in a word, his *philology*. The sun of Nietzsche's philology must shine with a radiant illumination upon the philosophic art works of Richard Wagner. Nietzsche's learning must serve Wagner's genius.

Just at this point, evidently, Wagner abandons a disinterested, unselfish friendship. He feels the necessity of making the conquest of his young partisan more and more complete. Accordingly, he writes Nietzsche this self-revealing, significant letter:

It is indeed a good thing to have such a correspondence as ours. I have at present nobody with whom I can talk things over as seriously as I can with you, my one friend. You might take from my shoulders much, even half of my life's business. You see on what a miserable footing I am with philology, and what a good thing it is that you are in the same position as to music. Now you will please remain a philologist in order to be led by music. I am in earnest about what I am saying. I beg you to show the benefit of philology and thus help me to bring about the great renascence.

It should be added, in this connection, that on Nietzsche's side his self-surrendering devotion does not seem to have been without struggle; we are never to forget his power of critical penetration and his sagacity. Even now, when most devoted, he perceived some of the weak points in Wagner's compositions, although he never alluded to them publicly. But the response, the echo, which Wagner's letter of exaction awoke in the heart of twenty-five-year-old Nietzsche, can readily be imagined. It was as if the very spirit of philosophy itself spoke to him and unveiled to him his mission. Nietzsche conceived his first philosophic work, if we may designate it a work inspired entirely by the philosophic impulse; he himself would have called it a centaur, an expression he was wont to use when speaking of works in which the artistic, metaphysical, and philological ways of looking at things were intertwined. The specific work in question was *The Birth of Tragedy out of the Spirit of Music*, elaborated from the autumn of 1869 until November, 1871, in a tranquil and peaceful time for Nietzsche, but also in months of war service and illness. The work was dedicated to Richard Wagner, *Meinem erhabenen Vorkämpfer*, and flung a bridge between the Wagnerian art and the Greek drama. It was such a cherishing of friendship as no other could offer to a master! It was a unique dedication,—loyalty to one's own self, loyalty to a friend, loyalty to the inner object of calling, the beloved Hellenism. Reverentially on New Year's Day, 1872, Nietzsche wrote the Goethe verse:

> Schaff, das Tagwerk meiner Hände,
> Grosser Geist, dass ich's Vollende!

The effect of the book upon the Wagner family was overpowering. It was born entirely from the Wagnerian world-view. It disclosed an understanding for that world-view from a new side, light falling from the Greek tragedy on the Wagnerian, and from the latter on the former. Interesting letters full of admiration came pouring from Liszt, from von Bülow, and from society women who were indefatigable and, of course, competitive, in serving Wagner's cause.

But the professional philologists ignored the book.

Nietzsche had made antiquity a living thing. An uncanny seriousness of life stared at them out of the book. The artistic-philosophic treatment broke over the fence of academic convention. Whole new problems were posed for the scholars, who thought that they had settled everything already. So the philologists either observed a significant silence, or else condemned the work.

Nietzsche's old patron, Professor Ritschl, after he had received a presentation copy, wrote to his former favorite:

You cannot complain much of me when I, the Alexandrine and scholar, oppose myself to a depreciation of perception and the intellect, and to a demand that one should see in art, and in art alone, the force which is to reform, redeem and free the world.

Nevertheless, the untiring vigor, the pulsing life in Nietzsche's book, which, with the sunlight of realities, shocked the men who studied in seclusion, and dazzled eyes spoilt by reading moldering Greek documents, of course entranced Wagner and his followers. They recognized the immense service which had been rendered to Wagner's art by this æsthetic, philological essay, in which Nietzsche's philosophical instinct led him to grope his way along a new path. "I have never yet read a finer book than yours! It is all magnificent!", Wagner wrote to his ardent apostle and defender. Similarly also wrote Frau Cosima.

The year 1872 saw many events in the life of Nietzsche. Bülow visited him, liked the book and the author, but would not allow Nietzsche to compose music. The progress of the scheme of Bayreuth made Wagner's presence there unavoidable, and in April, 1872, Tribschen days came to an end and the idyll became an epic. "Tribschen has now ceased to exist," wrote Nietzsche. "We walked about as amid ruins of the past. . . . Ah! it was desperate!"

In May, Nietzsche, Rohde and von Gersdorff stayed a few days in Bayreuth, when the foundation stone of the theater was laid. Here Nietzsche met the prominent Wagnerians, Baroness von Schleinitz, Countess Dönhoff, and especially Fräulein Malwida von Meysenbug, with whom he enjoyed a long friendship. "Those days," writes Nietzsche, "were simply wonderful, and the air was pregnant with something unutterable, something fraught with promise."

In June Nietzsche was in Munich with the Fräulein, hearing *Tristan und Isolde,* as conducted by Hans von Bülow. It was this same month that brought the first attack from the camp of the much-offended philology against her faithless follower Nietzsche, and against *The Birth of Tragedy,* the attack of the philologist von Wilamowitz, who abominated the amateur philosophy of Nietzsche and who aroused and pursued a violent polemic against him. Nietzsche's friends, Wagner included, defended him, for he himself considered self-defense beneath him. Rohde used cudgel and club and won a brilliant victory for Nietzsche. For all that, however, Nietzsche became outlawed and anathematized as a philologist. Students were advised to keep out of his classes: he had two students to whom he could lecture on rhetoric! "Stop dabbling in æsthetics and philosophy!" his colleagues demanded. "Keep to philology and let music alone!"

At this time, however, Nietzsche was slowly discovering the philosopher in himself. The philologist disappeared into the background. Philosophical instinct was too strong to be chained to the treadmill of a profession,—a professorship is not so bad if it were not for the teaching! Nothing could stop this instinct. Indestructible, in defiance of circumstances, it steered toward a predestined goal. Even his old idols—Schopenhauer and Wagner— were soon forsaken, after they had fulfilled their educational mission.

The Birth of Tragedy, which idolized and glorified his friend Wagner, having been written and published, Nietzsche, even then, almost imperceptibly, began to undergo a great change in his attitude toward him. It is important to remember what Nietzsche tells us in one of his prefaces, namely, that the great number of his writings express, not the feelings he experienced at the time he wrote them down, but the feelings already lived, which had given place in him to new ideas. This is why *Schopenhauer as Educator* is dated at a time when Nietzsche no longer believed in either Schopenhauer or pessimism. This is why *Richard Wagner at Bayreuth* was at bottom, to quote Nietzsche's fine sad words,

an acknowledgment of gratitude rendered to a moment of my past, to the beautiful period of a calm sea—and the most dangerous also of my existence . . . it was in reality a rupture, a farewell.

While, then, the period of self-surrendering devotion was drawing to its close, the old affection and the enthusiasm of the æsthetic again celebrated a triumph in the book, *Richard Wagner at Bayreuth,* but probably this drop scene was played contrary to the instincts and convictions of Nietzsche.

But I am anticipating my story. Wagner, when his friendship with Nietzsche was at high tide, wrote to him: "After my wife, you are the only joy life has brought." And again: "I swear to God, Nietzsche, you are the only one who knows what I strive for." This was fanaticism of friendship to which Nietzsche reacted with self-surrendering tenderness, abandoning a trip to Greece with Mendelssohn's son because it would give offense to Wagner. He even sought counsel as to how he might avoid offending Wagner when the latter was irritable. The friendship approaches high tide; the billows clamber up among the rocks, and cover them; but they cannot stay,—soon they go back to the sea, and the rocks appear, scarred and broken. It is low tide now!

Now follows the act of temptation. What introduced it? What sort of temptation could there be in such a relationship? Did the academic calling demand the release of the disciple from the bonds of the artist? Was the tempter vanity, or was it envy, which whispered to the young thinker: "You are too big to be the disciple of another, even of the greatest genius; break away, achieve the highest glory of a creator on your own account!"? Or, was it the soul of a Philistine which cried: "Come down from the summit; live in the valley more happily, more tranquilly!"? No, nothing of all this; the temptation lay in exactly the opposite direction. *Not to apostatize from Wagner, but to be true to himself*—that was Nietzsche's temptation. It was as this that Nietzsche perceived it. By "temper" we are wont to understand that principle which stimulates and misguides us to do wrong, to act counter to our better selves. Could this evil principle be present in our loyalty to our best friend? It could, indeed, if loyalty to friend be purchased only with the apostasy from something higher, if loyalty to something higher can be purchased only with apostasy to friend! Then loyalty to friend is disloyalty to the Socratic demon (*daimonion*) in our breast, is, in fact, temptation. It is in this shape that the tempter appears here. In view of what we already know, it need not be said that there could be for Nietzsche only one higher thing than loyalty to the master, and that this one higher thing was loyalty to the philosophic spirit, the *daimonion* of Socrates, in Nietzsche's own breast. But was not Wagner the incarnation of this philosophic spirit for Nietzsche, as, earlier, Schopenhauer was? Yes, *was,*—but not now: Wagner has ceased to represent that spirit. Just because Nietzsche was loyal only to the philosophic spirit in Wagner, just because Wagner was to him only the phenomenalizing, the objectivizing of that spirit, Nietzsche would have broken loyalty in this profoundest sense even to Wagner if he had maintained loyalty to him in the more superficial sense. Then would he have been loyal not to *friend* Wagner, but to the despiritualized shell, to an atomic complex. *Friend* Wagner was identically philosophic *spirit* Wagner. Disavowing the spirit, then, was disowning the friend! The conflict was terrible, especially terrible for so tender, so adoring, so grateful a nature as Nietzsche's. But the Wagnerian kingdom of this world, the Wagnerian promise that the angels of high society would see that poor Nietzsche would not dash his feet against a stone; the Wagnerian offer to make pessimistic stones into the bread of heaven, —these did not avail Nietzsche with his new demon, as they did not avail an earlier Nietzsche. And so both Nietzsches said: "Get thee behind me, Satan!" And yet we see him, in this second act, vibrating back and forth between two poles: the spirit of Bayreuth and the spirit of Philosophy. It is the old eternal struggle between Nirvana and Messiah, between resignation and *sursum corda,* between opportunism and principle, between "the flesh and the spirit," in the Pauline phrase. Nietzsche had his choice: Calvary or Bayreuth,—Calvary, rugged, naked, desolate, lonely, but keeping company with the sky; Bayreuth, sensuous, soft, sugary, medieval, murky, mephitic. And Nietzsche chose Calvary and the stars!

Nietzsche's fully conscious defection from Wagner's world-view begins in 1874. At this time he first lays the axe at the root of the tree of Wagnerian art. From this time on his disintegrating criticism inwardly advances farther and farther. I do not now refer to the objective grounds which led Nietzsche to depart from Wagner, but, to make the necessity of the personal breach intelligible, the reader must be reminded that Nietzsche was gradually strengthened in the development of his *Thoughts out of Season* into an independent thinker, that his own original views brought him to the decisive point in his opposition to Wagner. Wagner's goals turned ever more away *from* life; Nietzsche's *to* life. Wagner believed that the deepest truths unveiled themselves only in art, in metaphysics, in religion; Nietzsche now held more and more that scientific thought, purged of artistic, metaphysical, and religious prepossessions, was the vehicle of truth. Wagner surrendered to mysticism, Nietzsche to positivism. These were days when Nietzsche's soul was alone and full of tumult. Opposites in him were in conflict. Views of his own coinage were in violent deviation from those of his masters. This explains the Wagner situation, explains why

Nietzsche declined invitations from the Wagners, explains why Wagner's letters hurt him. It explains, on the other hand, his book, *Richard Wagner at Bayreuth,* wherein he assembled everything great that he had ever seen in the master, set him in a transfiguring light, sketched the ideal of an artist in dithyrambic tones—a radiant, vibrant, glowing picture—and called it Wagner! It was a great thankoffering to friendship, proffered with a bleeding heart. It was sent to the master shortly before the first Bayreuth festival, June, 1876. On July 12, 1876, Wagner wrote Nietzsche: "Friend! Your book is prodigious! How did you learn to know me so well? Come quickly, and get accustomed to the new impressions by attending the rehearsals. Yours, R. W." This is the last letter that Wagner ever wrote to Nietzsche.

But Nietzsche went to Bayreuth. The last and severest temptation now confronted him. The first fruit on the Bayreuth tree, to which Nietzsche had contributed, was now plucked. He could not stay away. Perhaps he hoped for the return of the old sincere days. But it was not to be. His Wagner ideal he had not discovered in Wagner, but had created out of his own soul. He was the victim of an illusion, an error. His doubt was confirmed. The catastrophe broke upon him. After the first rehearsal Nietzsche left the place, and buried himself for ten days in Klingenbrunn, deep in Bohemian forests. Here the great soul redeemed himself *to* himself, and to his inner veraciousness. Loyal to his philosophic spirit, he wrote *The Ploughshare,* the first elements of a new, free work.

But the beckon of Bayreuth was stronger for a last moment than the ban of his own thoughts. Once again he yielded to temptation and went suddenly back to Bayreuth. But this time, it was only an outer, not an inner return. Body, not soul, went. We shall never comprehend how deeply Nietzsche suffered during these weeks. It can be understood only by him whose most personal suffering and joy spring from his relation to an impersonal ideal.

Suddenly, in the midst of the festival, sick of its untruthfulness and obscurity, despite the fact that he had fallen in love there with an exceptionally fascinating and charming Parisienne, who, unfortunately, was already married, Nietzsche left Bayreuth finally, never to return. "The greatest event in my life," Nietzsche writes later, "was a recovery. Wagner was only one of my diseases." The temptation was now ended. The eagle had grown his wings.

We have now come to the third act: Nietzsche's victorious emancipation. From the first, he had differed from Schopenhauer on some essential points of doctrine. Later, he doubted the fundamental hypotheses of Schopenhauer's entire system, the attributes which Schopenhauer recognizes in the will, the will as essence of the world, the existence of a thing-in-itself. Soon he brushed aside the pessimistic conclusions of Schopenhauer's system: philosophic resignation and nihilism. On Wagner his judgment was not less free. He found that in *Die Walküre* serious defects must be weighed against marvelous beauty. To explain the intervention of the choir in Beethoven's *Ninth Symphony*, he outlined a theory which entirely contradicted that of Wagner. On another occasion he opposed to the Wagnerian conception of musical drama a radically different conception. Later, he noted what was immoderate in Wagner's gifts and character, and said that Bach and Beethoven showed "purer nature." He passed severe judgments upon Wagner's political life, on his relations with the revolutionists and the King of Bavaria, and on his anti-Semitism. He came to have significant doubts as to Wagner's value, not as an "integral" artist, but as a specialist: *i.e.,* as a musician, poet, dramatist, and even as a thinker. Especially did Nietzsche discover in Wagner certain "reactionary elements": sympathy for the Middle Ages, for Christianity, for Buddhism, for love of the marvelous, and for German patriotism. He was skeptical as to the real influence that Wagner could exercise in Germany. In short, while affirming that he was grateful to Wagner's music for "the purest happiness I have ever enjoyed," he showed plainly that he was a heretic in matters of Wagnerism at the very time when in public he covered Wagner with laurels. How can this apparent duplicity be explained?

Nietzsche gives the key to his conduct in these words:

At first we believe a particular philosopher. Then we say, if he errs in his manner of proving his statements, that these statements themselves are true nevertheless. Finally we conclude: his statements themselves are of indifferent value, but this man's nature is worth a hundred systems. As a teacher he may be wrong a thousand times; but his personality itself is always right, and it is that we should pay attention to. There is in a philosopher something that will never be in a philosophy; the cause of many philosophies,—genius.

Here, then, is the evolution of Nietzsche's feelings with regard to Wagner and Schopenhauer. Nietzsche began by becoming enamored of their works; then his love and respect were directed to the personalities of the authors;

finally, the moment came when he perceived that the differences which separated him from his masters were too great for him to be silent without exhibiting a want of sincerity toward himself; and, with deeply burdened heart, he obeyed the imperious exigencies of his conscience as thinker: he turned his criticism against his educators. He then saw that he had regarded them in a mistaken light. What he had sought for in them was not to understand them as they really were, but to understand himself by coming into touch with them. Instead of making himself like Schopenhauer and Wagner, as a disciple would do, he made Schopenhauer and Wagner after his own image and according to his own likeness, as a god does. Nietzsche's portrait of Schopenhauer gives, not Schopenhauer, but a Greek tragic philosopher. His portrait of Wagner gives, not Wagner, but the ideal figure of the Dionysian artist, —in a word, a kind of preliminary Zarathustra. Instead of painting his models, he described his own inward dreams, as he afterwards said in *Ecce Homo.*

At first he had accepted pessimism as a weapon against scientific optimism. The pessimistic criticism of the universe appeared to him to be the duty of every sincere man. On the other hand, he had never accepted without some reserve the nihilistic consequences which Schopenhauer drew from his premises: pity raised to a supreme virtue; the annihilation of the will to live proclaimed to be the final aim of existence. Absorbed at first in his battle against the Socratic culture of his age, Nietzsche did not take time to refute these nihilistic tendencies, or the Christian asceticism. But at length he saw that the nihilistic danger was as great as the optimistic danger, and that if the nineteenth century witnessed the flourishing of the mediocre and self-satisfied Philistine, it would be a century of decadence, tired of living, tired of suffering, aspiring to peace, to nothingness. A new problem then appeared to Nietzsche, a problem which never ceased to occupy his mind so long as he had a mind. What does this modern decadence consist of? What are the symptoms that characterize it, the signs that reveal it? What are the depth and breadth of the nihilistic evil? How can it be cured? Just as soon as the matter appeared to him in this light his judgments on Wagner and Schopenhauer were changed from top to bottom. His former allies in the war against optimism became his enemies in the war against pessimism, enemies dangerous in their fascination for him and his generation. If he had not shaken off their influence in time, he would never have arrived at the full knowledge of his own philosophy of the Superman.

The first chiming note of Nietzsche's own philosophy begins in *Human, all-too-Human,* written when Wagner wrote *Parsifal,* so disgusting to Nietzsche. The period of victorious enfranchisement was ended. Nietzsche says of his own book:

I thereby freed myself from all that did not belong to my nature; it is the monument of a crisis. It is the monument of a vigorous self-education, by which I put a sudden stop to all higher deceits, idealism, sense of beauty and the other woman-linesses which had infested me.

CHAPTER FOUR

Nietzsche and Feminism

This chapter will discuss, first, Nietzsche and Women; and second, Nietzsche and Woman. The first part will be practical and biographical; the second, theoretical and philosophic. One would like to know whether Nietzsche's experience with *women* accounts for his philosophy of *woman*. Or, does he borrow his beliefs in this regard from Schopenhauer? Or, again, are they to be explained as the consistent outgrowth from the very roots of his philosophy itself? This last is my own thesis, which I shall support at the proper place. Meantime, I am anxious to avail myself of any light upon the interesting problem which I may glean from the story of this remarkable man's life.

(1) *Nietzsche and Women*

It has already been pointed out that Nietzsche's father died when his son was but five years old; that Nietzsche was brought up by his mother, grandmother, and two maiden aunts; and that his only constant playmate was his loved sister Elizabeth. He spent his childhood, therefore, surrounded by exclusively feminine influences and guided by women's hands. Always in the company of his sister, always under the care of his mother and his aunts, he became somewhat feminine in his habits. Perhaps it should be said that these women were all very religious, their chief companions being German pastors. In her biography of "brother Fritz" his sister tells us that "he was the perfection of a well-mannered boy, and never did anything naughty."

But much later, in his first years at Bonn University, Nietzsche tried to convert himself into a beer-drinking, duel-fighting youth; and he owns that "the dash and pluck of fencing, the cheerfulness of beer feasts, the wantonness of bacchic songs, were some attraction to me for awhile." Soon, however, the vulgarity of thought and manners and morals nauseated the young man—"I could hardly endure certain individuals on account of their beer-materialism." He discontinued attendance at these social gatherings, and even left his club, writing a letter which it is worth while to reproduce:

October 20, 1865.

To the Students' Association, The Franconia:

I beg to inform the Association, the Franconia, that I herewith return it my sash, and, in so doing, send in my resignation. By this I do not mean to imply that I cease from valuing the principle of the Association. All I would frankly declare is, that its present features are not very pleasing to me. This may be in part my own fault; in any case it has proved a great effort for me to endure my membership over the year. Nevertheless, I regarded it as a duty to become acquainted with the Society, and now that no narrow bonds unite me with it, I bid it a hearty farewell.

May the Franconia soon grow out of that stage of development at which it now stands and may it ever claim highminded, moral men for its members.

FRIEDRICH NIETZSCHE.

Another incident belonging to this time reveals the soul of this man. He once paid a visit to Cologne by himself and was shown over the city by a servant. He asked the man to take him to a restaurant, but his guide misunderstood him and took him to a house of ill-fame. Deussen in his fine *Memoirs of Nietzsche* reports Nietzsche's account of the episode:

Suddenly I found myself surrounded by a half-dozen creatures in tinsel and gauze, who gazed at me expectantly; for a moment I stood absolutely dumbfounded in front of them; then, as if driven by instinct, I went to the piano, as to the only thing with a soul in the whole company, and struck one or two chords. The music quickened my limbs and in an instant I was out in the open.

The gulf which separated Nietzsche from those who were inferior to him in character thus early became apparent. While at first he joyfully entered into all the students' ways, joining their convivialities and taking part in their duels, his concern even in those days was solely with the things of the spirit: Greek tragedies; Schumann's *Faust* music; carrying a wreath to the composer's grave. At twenty-one, he wrote his friend Gersdorff, going through the same conflict at Göttingen: "A man has already lost a good deal when he has lost his moral indignation at the bad things which daily occur in his circle." Already, of course, Nietzsche was regarded as strange and abnormal by the rest of the students, was beginning to feel himself an alien among his comrades. Thus early he was treading the path of his pilgrimage into that melancholy aloneness which was to be his fatality, until at length he had to declare: "O, solitude, thou art my home!"

I have referred to these days to discover something of Nietzsche's soul. To return to the question of feminine contact and influence, let the reader consider this episode. The actress, Hedwig Raabe, was cheered in the most enthusiastic manner by full houses at Leipzig, to whose University Nietzsche had now gone. She was an enchanting artist. Nietzsche raved about her. He wrote an album of original poems and compositions in her honor. Lizzie writes: "Fritz was honestly in love with Hedwig Raabe, and Maximilian Harden is quite right when he says that she fulfilled the ideal of womanhood which my brother admired throughout the whole of his life."

The next matter of importance for our purpose finds Fritz passing under the influence of Schopenhauer. Lizzie did likewise; but Lizzie was thus confirmed in her ideal of personal salvation through renunciation and sacrifice for others. Fritz was hastened on, however, into his "atheism," such as it was, and, shall we say, into acceptance of Schopenhauer's views of women? I do not think so, although Lizzie says that he came back from Paris and Leipzig and sighed:

"Oh, Lizzie, life is really hard!" I did not understand the reason of this, as only just lately he had confided to me his happier view of life, as compared with Schopenhauer's pessimism. What then had happened? Was Fritz hopelessly in love, and had he met with difficulties about the betrothal? "What did you do in Leipzig?" I asked him one day with some caution. "I went for a walk," he replied. "Alone?" I inquired. "Oh, Lizzie," cried Fritz, "What a poor joke! Do you imagine I am going to become engaged? God forbid!"

He was then twenty-four years old.

And Lizzie goes on to say, in substance, that since Fritz had learned to know and honor Schopenhauer, he had expressed most dreadful views against women; that, as a matter of fact, he did keep rather aloof from women, "though he was full of the tenderest regard for them," Lizzie declares. "These extraordinary views of his," she writes, "therefore, seemed to be directed at a perfectly abstract being who had nothing whatever to do with us as a sex." He spoke of Frau Ritschl "in terms of the highest admiration"; . . . "in other respects his really fervent reverence for women was not at all in keeping with a disciple of Schopenhauer." He was very angry when doubt was expressed as to whether his "fair angel," Hedwig Raabe, "was really and truly an angel in character and manner of life."

Whatever Schopenhauer's influence upon Nietzsche's erotic life (and Schopenhauer was a gross realist in his attitude to women), it did not deter Nietzsche from proposing marriage now and then rather quixotically. In 1876, when he was not quite thirty-two, he proposed to a young Dutch girl, Fräulein Tr., "whom he had known only for a very short time and with whom he had taken a four hours' walk in Geneva. She was a charming girl, aspiring to good and lofty things, finding the epitome of her life's philosophy in Longfellow's *Excelsior*.' Nietzsche sent her a letter from which I quote below. A new acquaintance of Nietzsche's induced him to take this step— "a man who had known the girl a long while, who raved about her, and who subsequently married her":

My dear Young Lady:

This evening you are writing something for me [she was copying her translation of Longfellow's poem], and I will write something for you as well. Take your courage in both hands so as not to be too overcome by the question which I am now going to put to you: Will you be my wife? I love you, and it seems to me as if you already belonged to me. Not a word about the suddenness of my affection! In any case it is no sin, and therefore does not require to be pardoned. But what I should like to know is, whether you feel as I do—and that we never have been strangers at all, not for one moment! Do you not also believe that, joined together, each of us would be freer and better than we could be apart— therefore *Excelsior!* Would you dare walk shoulder to shoulder with me as with one who strives heartily after emancipation and improvement, along all the paths of life and of thought? . . .

To the young lady this offer of marriage proved too abrupt and disconcerting. Nietzsche wrote her again:

Dear Madam:

You are good enough to forgive me—this I feel from your very kind letter, which I really did not deserve. I have suffered so much at the thought of my cruel behavior that I cannot be sufficiently grateful to you for your gentle kindness. I shall explain nothing, nor do I know how to justify myself. I can only express this last wish, that if ever you should read my name, or meet me again, you will not think of the shock I have given you. I beg you ever to believe that I would fain make amends where I have erred.

With great respect, I am yours sincerely,

FRIEDRICH NIETZSCHE.

This was his first attempt at betrothal. Speaking of the matter a little later, he said: "I ought to be thankful for the way things turn out. A sudden, ill-advised marriage would in the end have been no better than a *marriage de convenance,* and from that may heaven preserve everyone!"

At about this same time his old friend Gersdorff wrote

that he had heard accidentally that another beautiful young woman loved and revered Nietzsche; that, as she was very wealthy, she was much sought after; and that she had already refused many offers for Nietzsche's sake. Right upon the heels of this other affair, however, the news came at the wrong time. Besides, Nietzsche was now busy pondering over the difficulties of marriage. On May 26, 1876, he answered:

I am not going to be married; as a matter of fact I so detest restrictions of any sort, and the thought of my adapting myself to the "civilized" order of things, that the woman could hardly be found who would be liberal-minded enough to follow me. I begin to regard Greek philosophers and their mode of life ever more and more as the proper examples to be followed.

I think that from this time on Nietzsche's intellectual plans and aspirations played by far the most important part in his life. It was impossible for him to regard love affairs as seriously as poets do, or to realize the part they played in other men's lives.

Nietzsche's best lifelong friend—friend only—among women, the motherly Fräulein Malwida von Meysenbug, urged him to marry to his pecuniary advantage and release himself from his professorship by finding a young lady whose highest ambition it would be to afford the philosopher Nietzsche an opportunity of carrying out his great life-work. Fräulein von Meysenbug went to work with a will at the program—wrote letters—asked girls how they felt about it—sought the coöperation of Nietzsche's sister. It seems that Nietzsche rather fell in with the plan at first. He wrote his sister during his illness, saying:

As soon as I got up Fräulein von Meysenbug took to her bed for three days, owing to rheumatism. Amid all our misery we laughed heartily together when I read her some chosen passages from your letter. . . . We are convinced that my professorial career in Bâle cannot be a permanent one; that I could only go on with it at the expense of all my more important projects. . . . After Easter, 1878, it will all be over, *if* the other combination succeeds,—that is to say, my marriage. The lady will have to suit my taste, but she must be well off—that is an essential. "Good, but rich," as Fräulein von Meysenbug said, and we laughed loudly at that "but." If I married, I should live the next few years in Rome—a most convenient place for health, for society, and for my studies. The matter is to be taken in hand this summer, in Switzerland, so that I can return as a married man to Bâle.

But the farther away from the motherly Fräulein he got, the more doubtful her program appeared. Afterwards he wrote his sister: "The proposed marriage is indeed an excellent idea, but most unlikely to be realized—of that I am certain."

Nietzsche gives a curious sketch of his state of mind at this time in a letter to Rohde, who had recently married:

Dear, dear friend, how shall I put it?—whenever I think of you, I am overcome with emotion; and when someone wrote to me the other day—"Rohde's young wife, a most charming lady, whose noble soul shines out in every feature," I went so far as to shed tears! . . . The other day, when I was mentally singing to myself my *"Hymn to Solitude,"* the thought suddenly came over me that you did not care a bit for my music and were very anxious to have a song on *"The Companionship of Two."* That same evening I played the song and succeeded—so that all the angels would gladly have listened, especially the human angels. But it was a dark room, with no one to hear; thus I had to keep all my happiness and tears to myself.

It is difficult to do full justice to the Salomé episode or to her book on Nietzsche. There is a long section on the subject in his sister's biography of him. Suffice it to say that Malwida von Meysenbug and Dr. Rée promised Nietzsche what he was looking for, a disciple, a certain Fräulein Lou Salomé, whom they considered peculiarly fitted to be taught his philosophy. According to them she was exceedingly clever and highly gifted and Nietzsche was expected to find in her a personality to whom he might bequeath the mission of expanding and spreading his teachings—a work which could be done far better by a living and devoted disciple than by books and writings. Nietzsche was greatly pleased, but the whole episode of his connection with this lady was destined only to cause unhappiness.

Fräulein Salomé came to Nietzsche and the initiation began, but Nietzsche soon discovered that she was not what he expected. It is almost impossible to sift thoroughly the details of this tragedy of errors, so as to impute justly guilt and innocence. This much is certain— that Fräulein Salomé, who was, after all, a woman with a heart, was bored by her position as a disciple. Nietzsche sublimated too much the idea of love. His sister, also, is not without blame in the matter. She, the respectable clergyman's daughter, often experienced difficulties in dealing with her impulsive and daring brother's mental flights. Fräulein Salomé poured out her grief in letters to friends. A letter from Dr. Rée, who seems to have sympathized with her, and of whom she was very fond, caused a scene between her and Nietzsche's sister, and was the beginning of a permanent rupture. The personal acquaintance lasted but five months. The philosopher's feelings were deeply wounded, and he was bitterly disappointed. It was too much for him to be compelled to relinquish the hope of a disciple. Fräulein Salomé, afterwards Frau Professor Lou Andreas-Salomé, later published the book on Nietzsche to which I have referred—a book of which his sister Lizzie says: "It can only be regarded as a product of injured feminine vanity revenging itself upon a poor invalid who could no longer defend himself." I quote Lizzie further: "In her anger, she revealed the ugly side of her nature: for instance, her petty annoyance at the refusal of Rée and Nietzsche to marry her, a refusal which she attributed to the lowest motives. . . . Her manner of expressing herself was simply revolting. . . . Perhaps Fräulein Salomé was only a forerunner of a certain section of the modern emancipated women."

Nietzsche's real opinion about her finds vent in a letter to Rée, from which I quote a sentence or two:

I thought I had found a person capable of *helping* me; which required, indeed, not only a lofty intellect but a morality of the first order. Instead of this, we have discovered a creature who merely wants to amuse herself, and is shameless enough to imagine that the greatest geniuses of earth are fit objects for her sport. . . . She told me herself that she had no morals (I thought that, like me, she had *stricter* morals than anyone else!) and that every day and every hour, she brought her God some sacrifice from herself.

For the rest, let the reader consult Nietzsche's "Grave song" in *Zarathustra,*—sad, softened memories of bitter days!

There remains Cosima Wagner. C. A. Bernoulli assumes that Frau Wagner was the one woman from whom Nietzsche's soul never freed itself; for here woman had met him as principle, as sphinx, as demon, as siren; and as his expiring age-consciousness merged itself into the Dionysos-incarnation, the ineffaceable shadow of this woman became to him the vision of the Dionysos-bride Ariadne.

At all events, in January, 1889, he wrote a note to Cosima from Turin—"Ariadne, I love you! Dionysos." Brief, but to the point! And there are those who think that Nietzsche's break with Wagner was due to this matter—that Nietzsche fled through fear of himself. But Lizzie says *no:*

Cosima personally was far from being the ideal woman who might have carried my brother off his feet in a torrent of passion. She was very tall and thin, her nose and mouth were far too large, and she could laugh, or at any rate her laughter sounded most unpleasant, so that she usually smiled instead. All these qualities were at variance with the graceful type which my brother admired, and which he always summed up in the phrase "a sweet little woman."

In the foregoing paragraphs I have sought to delineate, not all of Nietzsche's experiences with women, but all the *kinds* of that experience. We may turn now to his theory of woman.

(2) *Nietzsche and Woman*

Does Nietzsche's theory of woman grow out of Schopenhauer's philosophy, or is it a consistent product of Nietzsche's own basic views of life and of nature? The facts compel us to support, for the most part, the latter of these hypotheses. But I wish to say a word about the other two. Max Dielke asserts that Nietzsche is the greatest contemner or scorner of women among all German philosophers and authors. As against this assertion, it is my opinion that this unenviable distinction belongs to Schopenhauer. There can be no doubt that Schopenhauer was jealous—uncontrolled in his moods—boorish in his manners—that his egotism was all-consuming. His views on women were increasingly cynical. Schopenhauer's nature was strongly sensual. His amorous experience was not such as to nurture the growth of fine feeling or noble thoughts on the relation of the sexes. The truth is that Schopenhauer was fatally blind to all but the physical side of sex life. The subject is not one that he passes over with indifference, for it amounts almost to an obsession with him. Indeed, he left behind him notes on love and marriage which were held by his literary executor to be unfit for publication and were burned accordingly. Instead of being like this, Nietzsche was the very opposite. That his was a fine and tender nature is shown in his relations with women. That he followed the example of Schopenhauer and exhibited a bitter contempt for all women is not only a legend, it is a myth. Critics quote two cruel phrases from Nietzsche—the one: "Goest thou to woman? Forget not thy whip!" But surely "whip" is figurative, and not literal, and of its meaning more will be said later. The other passage reads: "A *learned* woman must have some physiological disorder"—some sexual privation. Is that such a bad thing to say? There are others besides Nietzsche that say it. Is that to say anything against woman as *woman?* To be sure, there is a type of woman whom Nietzsche thoroughly and cordially disliked, whom he abuses in words, the advanced and emancipated type, who would compete with man in the market place and in the laboratory; but if he reviles the lady clerk ("clerkess," he says) he is, on the other hand, full of innate and artless respect, full of sincere tenderness, for the eternal feminine, such as he conceived her to be. And Nietzsche seems to have accorded this instinctive respect to the women whom he met in private life. To the young woman whose acquaintance he made at Bayreuth he wrote letters of penetrating charm and exquisite delicacy. Nietzsche's soul was not Schopenhauer's soul, and Nietzsche's sentiment and attitude toward woman were not as Schopenhauer's.

Was Nietzsche's theory, then, due to his own experience? There are two considerations which might lead one to this opinion. For one thing, Nietzsche was a most personal thinker. It was an experience his very own that led him to say: "Every philosophy is its author's self-cognition." He also declared: "There is nothing at all impersonal in a philosopher." Hence he thinks that his books are no customary books: they are experiences—the *erlebtesten* books—experience of a thinker, of course; thoughts as experience. This being the case, it would seem that his views of woman must have an experiential origin. But when it is remembered that it is the experience of a thinker rather than of a liver, one's conclusion is accordingly modified.

The second consideration which could lead to the conclusion that Nietzsche's woman-views are due to Nietzsche's life, is this: It is not quite clear that he ever knew the "grand passion" itself. His sister says that he never knew either great love or vulgar love. I quote an important word from her: "My brother's only passion was the search for truth, and he exhibited little concern for anything else. He was greatly provoked when, later in life, he could never rise to the height of passion-love, but all his fancies for one of the opposite sex, however charming she might be, were rapidly transformed into a cordial friendship and nothing more."

In practice, then, his love was friendship. He himself says in theory: "Marriage should be a friendship, a means of strengthening our own ideal through another ideal; each should see the other's ideal from his or her own!" Again, he says: "The best element in marriage is friendship. If that friendship is strong enough, it has power to look beyond and even ignore the sexual aspect. Without friendship, marriage makes both parties small-minded and contemptuous."

According to Nietzsche's views, then, the most desirable basis for a marriage would not be "falling in love," but a deep friendship—a theory which *could* grow out of his experience. In this connection, certain jottings among notes in the Nietzsche archives will be of interest:

For the future of marriage: I argue burdens to be laid on bachelors more than on others as regards both taxation and military service. Privilege of all kinds for fathers of large families; under circumstances, a plurality of votes. A medical certificate to be required before every marriage, countersigned by the local authorities. As an antidote to prostitution [1] (or as a means of ennobling prostitution), there must be temporary marriages, legalized for a period of years or months, with a guarantee for the children; trustworthy members of the community to stand sponsors for every marriage.

[1] Mobius and Overbeck say that Nietzsche's view of woman was due to his association with demimondaine and prostitutes. Not so! In 1886, he wrote: "I have never desecrated the name of love."

But all this does not go to the root of the matter. I am myself satisfied that Nietzsche's fundamental conception of woman is rooted in the basic principles of his philosophy, and in this alone—neither in Schopenhauer, nor in his private experiences.

Nietzsche—this is the crucial point—holds that there is *a natural inequality between man and woman, and that it is a crime against life to convert this natural inequality into an artificial equality.* In other words, Nietzsche is for woman but against feminism, that is, the feminist movement, "woman's rights," so called. He would say that the so-called *feminism* of woman is the *masculinism* of woman, which is a crime against nature and against life. My contention is that this theory of Nietzsche's is grounded in the very principles of his philosophy, and this I now wish to show.

But what more definitely is Nietzsche's view of woman? If I were to select the two most characteristic passages from his writings on the subject, they would not be the two quoted above, the two which seem to be all that his adverse critics know, but rather these two: "Man's happiness is: I will. Woman's happiness is: He will." (*Zarathustra:* "Old and Young Women.") The other is as follows: "Everything in the life of woman is an enigma, and everything in woman has a solution which is called 'childbirth.'" These give the gist of his view. And so, his execrations and his most furious sarcasms are directed against the emancipated woman, who has lost both the fear and the respect of man, who can no longer give herself up to him, but insists on treating him as an equal; who resents the homage and consideration of the sterner sex toward weaker woman as an insult; who would even compete with him in the struggle for life. Nothing is more hateful to him than the bluestocking who would take part in literature, science or politics, except, perhaps, the lady clerk, who in this modern society (in which the industrial spirit has gotten the better of the artistic and warlike spirit), aspires to judicial and economic independence; protests loudly against the state of slavery in which she is held, and organizes noisy campaigns to obtain rights equal to those of man. Nietzsche, indeed, believes that woman's influence decreases as her so-called rights increase. He cautions women that they are taking a false step in trying to be rivals of men; that they are on the point of losing their influence, and of lowering themselves in public esteem. It is to the interest of women to appear to men as beings of entirely different nature, afar off and inaccessible, difficult to understand and to govern, vaguely formidable, but also frail, worthy to be pitied, and requiring an infinite amount of consideration. But women themselves are now throwing off this mysterious halo; they are unlearning feminine modesty—ready as this modesty once was to be aroused—by contact with all kinds of ugly or vulgar reality. Mingling freely with the multitude, even striving to elbow her own way through the mob of egotistic appetites, woman is *depoetizing* herself! And at the same time woman is wearing herself out nervously under the pretext of artistic culture; she is losing her nerves—especially by the abuse of Wagnerian music! And she is thus becoming unfit for her natural vocation, which is the bringing of fine children into the world.

That is the gist of Nietzsche's thought about woman. Perhaps I ought to express it a little more "brutally"—as the feminist would say—as follows: Nietzsche stands for

by nature must assert himself as stronger. All leveling systems, all emancipating ideas, issue from thoughts contrary to the laws of life. Because feminism necessarily links itself with this antinaturality, Nietzsche condemns it, while he paints the worth of woman *qua* woman in luminous and ravishing colors.

The two thoughts are reconcilable: the inner, the philosophical thought of the relation of the sexes under the optic of the elevation of the type man is illuminated on two sides. Woman is not end, but means. Will she be self-end?—she must be pushed back into her place energetically. As means, however, woman is the noblest instrument of strength; strength finds rest and repose in woman's love. All the longing of woman is: May I be the mother of the Superman?

CHAPTER FIVE

NIETZSCHE AND THE STATE

WHAT ideas did Nietzsche possess and preach concerning government—Spartan Nietzsche, the storm-swept genius of the Upper Engadine, the fiery spirit of whose teachings tastes like a tonic when we are sick of the mush of benevolent mediocrity; Nietzsche, the hater of democracy and Christianity as the two great sentimentalisms of history—both misleading mankind, seducing social and political thinkers from the hard upward path which involves submission to scientific fact and the interpretation of history in the light of biology? Saint Francis of the Church and saintless Rousseau of the State, these, to Nietzsche, are two of the greatest betrayers of humanity, who unconsciously encourage man to prefer sentiment to truth, the soft fallacies of the heart to the hard facts of experience and of life. We must not lose sight of Nietzsche's gospel of uncompromising, strenuous, disciplined aristocracy, an aristocracy that will not flatter the masses by pretending that it is their servant; that will, so far as it is necessary for its own development, pitilessly, although not cruelly, exploit the masses, by the law of self-expansion innate in its own being. Nietzsche urged self-assertion rather than self-sacrifice, recognized will and instinct as the underlying, driving forces of life and denied, as against Shelley, intellect and idea as constituting the inner springs of the machine. He refused to idealize "the people," finding that the people could drink too much, and gamble, and be lazy and tell lies as well as their so-called betters. Like Moses, Nietzsche had to create the very taste for the freedom which he sought to satisfy; like Moses, he wondered whether the people were worth the sacrifice that was being made for them.

In former chapters we have seen something of the higher Nietzscheanism which would base the obedience of the masses on the conscious or unconscious conviction that only in acknowledging nature's choice of supermen as autocratic leaders lies salvation from anarchy and from the decline of all really civilized life. But the Superman in this conception is a Hercules bearing the new world on his shoulders, not a mere Colossus straddling over it. Nietzsche taught that it was no gain to exchange caste for the reign of the average, for the dislike of littleness to believe that anywhere in the world there exists anything except the tame and the mediocre; for the resenting, on the part of the small in mind, of all height and depth, range and mystery, expression of the dull hate of the commonplace for variety and distinction, for adventure and experiment. Yet Nietzsche was not a mere apostle of selfish and unscrupulous force; not the prophet of the "blond beast" with fang and claw, but without brain and will; he was the preparer of the way for the coming race rulers, bound to arrive if wisely prepared for; in a word, Nietzsche was the evangelist of aristocracy and eugenics.

If in the foregoing paragraphs, I have lauded Nietzsche, it has been with a view of creating tonic atmosphere, of stimulating my "readers" imaginative response, without which it were not worth while to interpret him at all. We are now above vulgarity of mind, above slavery to mediocrity and the commonplace, to vice and stupidity. We have been to Upper Engadine and have beheld there the rainbows and bridges of the Superman: in such a mind and mood we may most successfully commune with the soul of Friedrich Nietzsche.

The exaltation of the State—did Nietzsche stand for that? Were Nietzscheanism and Prussianism entirely at one? Was Nietzsche purely a militarist or not? Was his contempt for the self-governing capacity of the multitude complete or not? Did Nietzsche think that in war-time, the multitude had no other function than to prepare to act as cannon fodder at their master's bidding? Would he have had any sympathy at all with this private letter about the Great War, from an Irish Catholic working girl: "But," she writes, "But, oh worst of all, the tremendous slaughter of human life. Those who have caused the image of the Great God to be ruthlessly sacrificed in this manner will assuredly receive an awful punishment at His hand." What would Nietzsche think of the spirit and temper and principle of that letter? Then we talk much of collective life to-day, of the crowd-mind, or the organism of society as a whole, of a "wise collectivism" which recognizes individuality indeed, but not individualism. Life, we declare, is an organism and not a collection of atoms. What would Nietzsche say to all that—would he be with us or not?

Some of us say that the Prussian obsession of militarism is not to be met by our lack of a collective ideal, or of a conception of the State as a common life or corporeity. Some men say that the way of avoiding the Prussian obsession is not to leave individuals in supposed freedom to be exploited by either Mammon or Moloch. Mammon, the money-power, the evil genius of democracy: Moloch, the war god, the evil genius of the disciplined military state of Imperial Germany. Is the master of men everlastingly to be either, Mammon or Moloch? What does Nietzsche think? After the battle of Jena, Prussia, during her wonderful revival, did not accept Hegel's view of the State as an organism, but made force the State's characteristic feature. Did Nietzsche fall in with that program? Did he hold that the State was superior to, something more than, the sum of the individuals that compose it? What would Nietzsche think of the middle-class English notion, still more of our American notion, that a State consists of a voluntary consensus of independent individuals concurring, so far as they do concur in certain objects, but at bottom claiming the right for each one to do as he likes, rejecting any idea of standards of universal acceptance? What would Nietzsche think of the worship of the State with the negation of humanity, the cult of an abstraction, the idea that the individual exists for the sake of the State, not the State for the individual?

Or, finally, did Nietzsche ever come to think that the State was a nuisance, a menace to the dignity and liberty of the unfolding human spirit? It is difficult to read Nietzsche without being disturbed by such questions as these.

Aside from what Nietzsche himself has to say, I shall refer briefly to the history of the evolution of the State. In the transition from *nature* to *culture,* we first have primitive man, representing the lowest grade of culture, a tribal culture at best. His weapon, bow and arrow, was made for hunting, not war. Primitive man does not engage in tribal wars—there is only the strife of individual with individual. Primitive life was not a war of all against all, as Thomas Hobbes described it. The facts are just the opposite. The natural condition was one of peace. The tribes that have remained relatively primitive to this day led a peaceful existence since immemorial times.

Succeeding the primitive era, we have, secondly, the totemistic age—to us, a submerged world. Here man does not have dominion over the animal, but the animal rules man. The deeds and activities of animals cause fear, wonder, and adoration. The souls of the dead dwell in animals. Animals become the ancestors of men. The totemic idea affects the organization of society. There are tribal division, the forms of marriage, and the family, but there is as yet no State.

Totemic culture is succeeded by a third period, the age of heroes and gods. To be sure, initial steps toward this age were taken in the totemistic period, in the development of a rulership of individuals within the tribal organization. This rulership was first temporary, then it became permanent. The position of the chieftain was only of minor importance in the totemistic age. But—and this is the essential matter—the chieftain gains in power when the tribal community assumes a military organization under the pressure of struggles with hostile tribes. Society thus develops into the State. The guidance of the State in times of peace, certainly, but war especially, calls out men who tower far above the stature of the old chieftains. In place of the eldest of the clan and the tribal chieftain, this new age gives rise to the *hero*. The totemistic age possesses only fabulous narratives—myths—dealing with animal ancestors who have introduced fire, taught the preparation of food, etc. The hero who is exalted as a leader in war belongs to a different world, a world faithfully mirrored in the heroic song and epic. As regards their station in life, the heroes of Homer are still essentially tribal chieftains; but the enlarged field of struggle and the magnified characteristics which it develops exalt the leader into a hero. With the rise of poetry, the forms of language also change and become enriched. The epic is followed by plastic and dramatic art. All this is closely bound up with the origin of the State. The State now displaces the more primitive tribal institutions, and national religions come into being, with national heroes and with states. As the hero is the ideal man, so the god becomes the ideal hero.

The primitive, the totemistic, the heroic ages—these are, or rather are to be, succeeded by a fourth period, the humanistic. A national state and a national religion do not represent the permanent bounds of human striving. National affiliations are to broaden into humanistic associations. As the fisherman's hut, in Goethe's tale, widens into the temple of the universe, so our state politics of this people and that people are to widen into the planet-politics of all mankind. This is a development in which we of the present generation are beginning to participate. As yet it is not, but it is coming to be. We can speak only of an advance *toward* humanity, not yet of a development *of* humanity. The primitive, the totemistic, the heroic, the humanistic!—this is the long human story. Each successive era has retained something from all the preceding. The family and marriage are legacies from primitive and totemistic life. Will the future discard them, valuable once but worthless hereafter? Similarly, the State is a legacy from the third, the heroic age. Will the future humanism discard the State? Will it be impossible for this age of humanity, the fourth age, ever to dispense with the more limited articulations of state and society that have arisen in the course of cultural development? Or, just as there is a food instinct, a sex instinct, as important to-day as ever, is there a State instinct? The clan had no idea of becoming a State, as primitive man and woman had no idea of becoming parents and family. The ancient demon-belief did not intend to become god-belief. Is there then a State instinct, so that the State is as firmly and deeply rooted biologically as food- and sex- and god-instincts? As the latter push up and abide in the fourth period of humanity, so will the former?

Whatever be the truth it is certain that the idea of the State must change from that of the *ruler* of humanity of the third era, to that of the *servant* of humanity of the fourth era. The hero with his domination, must yield to the servant, with his ministry. The so-called rulers of the Gentiles lord it over them and their great men overbear them, said Christ—not so with you: "Whosoever wants to be great among you, must be your servant." There is no Mammon-money-god or Moloch-war-god in that!

No, if the State continues, it has got to change. The State has got to cease to be something outside the people—whether oppressive or paternal. It must be the body of which they are organically a part. The State must become the firm of which all the members of the nation, by the very character of race and birth, by the assurance of the blood circulating in their veins, have by right incorporate membership, are "citizens of no mean city." All exploiting, therefore, of some classes by others more favorably circumstanced is an offense against this common life, and it is the business and interest of the State to render impossible such exploiting in the interests of its own well-being, which means that all its citizens should be the best possible citizens in mind and body, and none merely used as instruments for other's good.

But what we must here insist upon is that the State is the characteristic mental creation of that third era—the era of heroes and gods.

Nietzsche declared that the gods are dead. But what of the hero? What does the prophet or the Superman say? What is Nietzsche's attitude to the State in its former function of ruler and authority—autocratic; or in its modern or future function of servant—democratic, socialistic? It is only against this background of history and theory that his thought can be helpfully interpreted.

Nietzsche's chief utterances on this subject are to be found in the following of his books:

(a) *Early Greek Philosophy* ("The Necessity of Slavery").

(b) *The Future of Educational Institutions* (Here he discusses public schools and Hegelian philosophy, culture, State as guiding star to culture).

(c) *Thoughts out of Season*, Volume I, speaks of the State founded upon music; Volume II, discusses service of the State as the highest end of man.

(d) Especially *Human, all-too-Human*, Volume I, "A Glance at the State."

(e) *The Dawn of Day* speaks of the State as the production of anarchists.

(f) *Thus Spake Zarathustra* (Probably the most terrific arraignment and anathema of the State in all literature).

(g) *The Genealogy of Morals,* in which the origin of the State is discussed.

In former chapters it was shown that the central point of Nietzsche's philosophy is a lyrical and enthusiastic affirmation of life; of life beautiful, strong, exuberant, overflowing; of life manifesting itself, variously and vividly, in art, and in social, intellectual, political, administrative activity; of life in all its plenitude and power.

But Nietzsche saw so many obstacles to the realization of this ideal—the ideal of the Superman. These obstacles were the institutions of the present day, institutions in some cases so ancient and venerable as to be taken for axiomatic truth. But these institutions did not spring up fortuitously or arbitrarily: they are rooted in the habits, prejudices, and traditions of the race, hence in the psychology of the individuals composing the race. Similarly, many of the obstacles in question are inherent in the habits, traditions, and prejudices of humanity.

For instance, there is the feeling of fear before the unknown. Humanity does not like to explore the virgin forests, which threaten the bold wanderer with a thousand perils. The sentiment of fear before the unknown is an obstacle to the free and unfettered search after knowledge. Man must shake off this fear. He must unlearn a great deal—throw off the burdens of morality, of religion, of the State, and all other obstacles to the realization of his integral self. But how many care to face this risk? How many care to wander through the labyrinths of virgin forests or navigate amid the reefs of unknown seas in order to attain to the bottom of things,—if they have a bottom?

Nevertheless, the risk must be faced bravely—no matter what the disappointments, mortifications, deceptions. Among these obstacles we have the State. Nietzsche came at last to hate the State. To him, *the State is synonymous with mediocrity organized*. It is the invention of the weak. It aims at the suppression of the strong, the gifted. The logical expression of the State is democracy, with its absurd doctrine of equality. The aim of the modern State is not the development of the individual, not the creation of beauty, not the cultivation of a superior race, not even the protection of the better and stronger elements in a race. The aim of the State is the greatest possible multiplication of individuals, the suppression of all that is exceptional and superior to the mass. In a word, the aim of the State is the greatest happiness of the greatest number.

And so, according to Nietzsche, the State, the modern State, is the creation of the weak, by the weak, for the weak. I quote from *Thus Spake Zarathustra* ("The New Idol"):

The State? What is that? I will open my ears, and I will recount you the story of the death of nations. The State is the coldest of all cold monsters. It lies coldly, and this is the lie which proceeds from its mouth: "I, the State, am also the People." But it is a lie. They were creators, those that created the different peoples and gave them a faith and an ideal: And thus did they serve life.

They are destroyers and nihilists, those that set traps for great numbers and call those traps the State; they hang a sword and a hundred passions above them. There where a strong race still exists the State is not understood, and is hated as an evil eye and as a crime against morals and liberty. The State lies with all the tongues of good and of evil; and whatever proceeds from it is a lie, and all that it possesses is stolen. Everything connected with the State is false; it bites with stolen teeth, and its very bowels are false.

Being an instrument designed to permit of the greatest possible multiplication of individuals, the State necessarily tends to favor the increase of numbers of wholly superfluous persons—and so Nietzsche continues (in *Zarathustra*):

The State—there where are all the drinkers of poison, good and bad. It is there where all, good and bad, lose themselves. It is there where the slow suicide of all is termed "life."

Behold these superfluities! They steal the work of the discoverers, and the treasures of the wise. They call their theft education—and everything in their hands becomes illness and impotency!

Behold these superfluities! They are forever ailing, they give vent to their spleen and call the result their newspapers. They devour each other, but cannot even digest each other.

Behold these superfluities! They make wealth and yet become poorer, and first of all that condition precedent to all power—money!——

*　　*　　*　　*

There, where the State ceases to be, there begins the man who is not superfluous. There where the State ceases to exist—behold, my brethren! Do you not see the rainbow and bridge of the Superman?

The State, then, whether autocratic or democratic, is always the enemy of everything which is exceptional, of everything which is powerful, of everything which rises above the ordinary, of everything which is independent. What the State aims at is the multiplication and the protection of the inferior elements of the race, elements which constitute the State's strength and guarantee its longevity. In one word—*the State loves correct attitudes,—normality, mediocrity!*

The proof? All those who rule humanity with a rod of iron have either broken loose from all State control, or else have used the machinery of the State in order to assert their powers. The State is a tool in the hands of Cesare Borgia, Peter the Great, Napoleon—a tool for dominating the masses; the masses need the State to protect them against exterior force—against themselves even. The State, like the religions, acts as policemen act who prevent the bad instincts of the masses from breaking loose.

We must now discuss a matter which is not usually understood. The position of Nietzsche in regard to the State is fundamentally opposed to the position of the anarchists who claim him. The anarchist desires the abolition of the State in order to do away with the power of the governing classes—of the bourgeois and capitalist classes—in order to ensure to each worker the integral value of his own production; in order to abolish the exploitation of the industrious working classes by the capitalists and employers. According to the anarchist theory, the State is the instrument of class domination—the means whereby the capitalist class is able to prolong its domination—the great obstacle which prevents the realization of the anarchist ideal of universal fraternity and solidarity.

The difference between Nietzsche and the anarchists is this: The anarchist has as a starting point the ideal of a humanity living in peace, fraternity, and solidarity—a humanity whose unit, the individual, is naturally good, naturally pacific. But this natural goodness and peace, he thinks, have been, for the time, destroyed by various influences, of which the State is the most important.

Nietzsche, on the contrary, has as a starting point the ideal of a humanity living in strife and in war, of a Superman dominating humanity by his strength, a Superman strong, ferocious, merciless. He sees in man, a creature not naturally good, but vicious; he sees in the State, not the destroyer of man's "good" qualities, but the destroyer of his passions and of his "vices," of what is fundamental and attractive in human nature.

The anarchist school hates the State as a symbol of power; Nietzsche hates the State as a symbol of weakness. The anarchist school heralds the downfall of the State as the end of tyranny; Nietzsche sees in the downfall of the State the means of establishing the dominion of the Superman.

The anarchist school works against the State as an instrument of class domination, and asserts the interest of the masses; Nietzsche thunders against the State as an instrument for the protection and creation of the masses and asserts the interest not of the masses but of the Superman.

Anarchist and Nietzsche agree in desiring the downfall of the State, then, but for entirely opposite reasons. The anarchist school desires the complete downfall of the State in order to inaugurate the era of anarchy.

But what is more precisely Nietzsche's position? Perhaps, after all, Nietzsche does not desire so complete a downfall of the State as we might imagine. Nietzsche is an autocrat. So far as the State represents authority, that is, the Will to Power, to dominate, Nietzsche is perhaps willing to accept it.

"But," my reader may reply, "this is precisely what the State does represent, authority versus anarchy!" This is to misunderstand Nietzsche's conception of authority, and also of the authority of the State. We must never forget that Nietzsche is an autocrat, an enemy of the democratic ideal,—an autocrat who aims at the establishment of an autocracy which shall govern by reason of its strength, its power, the terror and awe and respect and veneration which it inspires. The Nietzschean autocracy is to be one to which only the fittest shall be admitted, creators of the values which humanity worships, and each member shall conquer admittance only by his deeds of daring and prowess, intellectual and physical, *which no State could permit,* for such deeds would destroy the State and falsify its aim and *raison d'être.* Here I shall quote one of Nietzsche's most striking sentences:

In our present civilized world we know only the degenerate criminal, crushed by the hostility and contempt of society— the criminal who distrusts himself, who often seeks to belittle and excuse his act,—in short, a type of criminal who has failed; and we forget that every great man was a criminal, only not in miserable style, but in great style; we forget that every great act is a crime.

According to Nietzsche, the great man, the hero of the future, worthy to be master and ruler of men must necessarily be a criminal,—that is to say, a man who knows not good or bad, because he is above them; a man who is the scourge of humanity; a man who, in order to realize the expansion of his personality, needs humanity as a field of experiments, as a field in which he can sow suffering broadcast; a man warlike and hard-hearted; "Be hard!"

Nietzsche says. The aim of the Superman is a great aim; it is the realization of life in its fulness and entirety, in all its infinite possibilities; and in the great game which the Superman plays with destiny humanity is but a pawn! Authority of blood and iron,—that is what Nietzsche would set up.

If we turn now to the State of to-day, whether it be autocratic or constitutional, we find that every act which qualifies for admittance into the autocracy of to-morrow is condemned. The State is moral—the Superman is immoral.

The object of the State is not the creation of beauty nor the development of individual power and independence. The object of the State is the development of mediocrity— the creation of a flat, colorless ideal of uniformity, not beautiful and not the symbol of strength.

The aim of the State is the "good" man, the "correct" man, the staid man of business, the placid and conservative "bourgeois, who lives within his income and leads an honorable, sedate, quiet, domestic life." The State inculcates respect of the law, the moral law also, enjoins the worship of the trinity of the Good, the Beautiful, the True. The State is the enemy of initiative and independence.

The State has been created to render the life of the greatest number tolerable—to curb and suppress the passions which surge up in the human soul, and which threaten the peace and good digestion of one's neighbors.

But an opponent might say to Nietzsche: "The State does nevertheless represent a principle of authority, and in order to obtain authority you must have power." Nietzsche would answer:

Certainly, the State possesses authority, but there are two kinds of authority: There is the authority obtained by the superabundance of force and energy, such as was realized in Napoleon. And there is also the authority which is obtained by all sorts of intrigue, backstairs plotting, cunning tricks, baseness, meanness, slyness, and such is the authority of the State. Those who to-day aspire to rule the State, not being strong enough, courageous enough, or bold enough, to assert their supremacy by strong, courageous, bold means, resort to all sorts of crooked and unclean methods. The results of the activity of the State have long been manifest. Biologists have repeatedly called attention to the growing degeneracy of the race, as the result of the policy consistently pursued by the governing class. Darwin was exceedingly pessimistic as to the future of the race. The race does not increase in strength [Nietzsche writes]; its weaklings are always triumphant over its strong man.

In summing Nietzsche's view, then, we find that he regards the State as a creation of the weaker elements of the race, who by dint of their greater cautiousness, slyness, deceit, trickery and self-possession, have succeeded in out-manœuvring the stronger and fiercer elements. The State is the instrument of the protection of these weak and treacherous elements. The rule of the State is the rule of jobbers and place hunters,—forced to resort to all manner of bribery, including the holding out of visions of the future which appeal to the worst passions of the masses, visions which tempt their cupidity and excite their malice and envy. The result of this dependence of the political place-holders on the masses is the enactment of legislative measures in the highest degree prejudicial to the well-being of the race as a whole, prejudicial to individual liberty and initiative, prejudicial to social progress or organization. The State, therefore, is one of the chief obstacles to the realization of that ideal of force, of beauty and of integral life, which Friedrich Nietzsche preached. Thus spake Zarathustra!

CHAPTER SIX

NIETZSCHE AND MILITARISM

NIETZSCHE was first artist, then scientist, then prophet. Since it is from the prophetic period that we derive most of his war literature, it is important to take into account his prophetic style and manner of utterance.

Certainly, Nietzsche is a craftsman of the first rank. He manipulates language with a rare virtuosity, and consciously avails himself of all of the means and devices of a brilliant style. He is rich in striking antitheses, in elaborate pictures, in pertinent coinages, as well as in unexpected plays upon words. He understands the art of inducing a cumulative effect even to the point of explosive violence, as well as the art of delicate allusion, of sudden dumbfounding and silence.

These properties of style emerge especially at the time when he began to write in aphorisms, in the compact brevity of which close attention to form is required. Nietzsche understood preëminently how to manipulate the rhetorical arts in his aphorisms. But quite apart from this, aphorisms as such are an effective device of style— single thoughts appear much more sharply and appealingly in their abrupt particularity than would be the case if they were soberly placed in their order and sequence, not grounded in the antecedent nor softened by the consequent. Each single thought appears in harsh one-sidedness, as if sprung from nothingness,—and this makes all the stronger impression. Let such short sayings be uttered with prophetic poignancy and dignity, and they force the reflective mind into activity far more effectively than long-winded argumentation could do.

Nietzsche speaks in such short, sharp precepts—like the founder of a religion. They are compressed texts, and everybody finds peculiar charm in making his own gloss for the texts. As I say, the first writings of Nietzsche do not show this form, but *neither do they speak of war.* Only since 1876 did he so write. It is a style in which literary people are inclined to accord him the uncontested palm of mastership.

And now, to this purely historical art and finesse of the aphorist, we must add the art of the lyric poet in Nietzsche. Others wrote polished aphorisms—La Rochefoucauld and Pascal, Lichtenberg and occasionally even Schopenhauer; but Nietzsche is more—he is a lyrist. This lyrical quality of his style shows itself in the emotions which he supplies, in the flow of passion with which he speaks, in the subjective coloring which everything assumes. An extremely temperamental ego speaks to us in all his utterances. In all those aphorisms we get the inner experience of the author, his personal joy and pain. This lyric element mounts to formally poetic altitudes occasionally;—prose fails him and Nietzsche seizes upon poetic form in the shape of the dithyramb. This is especially true of his *Zarathustra,* the glowing and profound lyric thought of which reminds us of Giordano Bruno and of Hölderlin.

But as we must add to the aphoristic the lyric, so we must add to the lyric the symbolistic. Symbolism especially characterizes Nietzsche's main work, *Zarathustra.*

The figure of Zarathustra himself and his story is symbol to Nietzsche, a poetic construction, a parable. In Zarathustra Nietzsche materializes himself (to use the language of spiritism) and his ideal: in the fate of Zarathustra we behold the necessary mutations and upheavals of his own nature, the dissonances and their resolutions in his own inner being. But this parable, in the case of Nietzsche, never becomes dry, didactic allegory, but remains living symbol. On the other hand, the parable is never too distinct and obtrusive, but remains always in the *clair-obscur* of the intimated, of the *dawn of day,* and so, of just the symbolic. And the *clair-obscur* of symbol rises occasionally to the heights of enigmatic mysticism, where deeper, more mysterious backgrounds are unveiled behind what is said.

It has been necessary to call attention at some length to this stylistic character of Nietzsche's writings, for if one forgets this style as Nietzsche treats of war, and of woman, and takes his words as prosaic, literal, matter-of-fact, scientific, and not aphoristic, lyric, symbolic, mystic, one will misunderstand many a passage and will fail to gain an insight into his true position on these and other subjects.

Before we go into the question of content, shall it be held that content is rooted in Nietzsche's *personality?* Should the personal characteristics of the man be disengaged? Perhaps it were better to do so, yet I hesitate, so great is the difference between a character sketch and real life! In Nietzsche's case it is quite certain that the philosophic impulse is the fountainhead from which his personality is to be understood. The delineation of the personality of Nietzsche, then, is tantamount to the delineation of the philosophic personality of Nietzsche. But the philosophic impulse can be preponderatingly understanding, theoretical thought, or feeling, or will—that is, it can make intellect, feeling or will serviceable, employ either as vehicle in order to live out this impulse in life. And so we have, in the one case, a *scientific* philosopher (Leibnitz, Wundt); in the next case, an *artist*-philosopher (Plato, Schopenhauer); in the third case, the *prophetic* philosopher (Pythagoras, Empedocles). Of course, a *scientific* philosopher investigates, establishes; an *artist*-philosopher feels and forms; the *prophetic* philosopher proclaims and demands and enlists. Now, master-thinkers belong predominantly to one or another of these groups. But of Nietzsche one cannot say this; for, to reiterate, now he is artist, now investigator, and now prophet—frequently all three at once—no one ever exclusively.

This *triplicity* is the most peculiar thing in Nietzsche's philosophic individuality. Perhaps this is the reason why neither as artist, nor as scholar, nor as prophet, Nietzsche quite became a star of the first magnitude. This triplicity in coördination of its factors is the reason again why we cannot describe the theoretical Nietzsche apart from the emotional Nietzsche, or *vice versa*. We must abandon the effort to understand the heart and head of Nietzsche sundered from each other. If now we seek the most important properties in which there is an interplay of the two, we shall find two things, which I choose to call intensity and finesse, or, more simply, *strength and fineness*. Strength and fineness,—these constitute the personality of Nietzsche. I agree with Mügge's striking phrase: *"Nietzsche's intellect was as hard as iron, but his heart was soft as down."*

Are the war utterances of Nietzsche to be interpreted from the point of view of the hardness of his intellect, or from that of the softness of his heart, or both? It is the union of this hardness and softness that accounts for the fanaticism of Nietzsche.

We shall have to supply another word, however, as to the relation between life and doctrine, man or personality and work, in the case of Nietzsche. Two erroneous views are current among us. One is the belief that the Superman is the enlarged portrait of Nietzsche himself; the other is the belief that the Superman is the exact opposite of Nietzsche and that therefore the work has nothing to do with the man. The first view is entirely wrong; we know that the higher type man, which Nietzsche would breed, is the hard, hilarious, pitiless master-man. But there is little of all this to be traced in the personality of Nietzsche. Nietzsche was himself—his intellect aside—effeminate, tender, devoted, affectionate, sympathetic. He warns his mother, sister, friends, not to read his writings, saying: "Every profound thinker fears more being *understood* than being misunderstood." His vanity may suffer from the latter, but from the former suffers his heart, his fellow feeling, which avers: "I would not have it as hard with you as with me." He was grieved that his attack upon Strauss caused the latter sorrow and perhaps death. He showed mildness, tenderest regard for friends, giving or lending money right and left. His eyes looked goodness or melancholy, not the divine wickedness and hilarity which he preached. His moral conduct was *bourgeois*. "Everything illegitimate is offensive to me," he writes.

But some take certain extremes in Nietzsche's doctrines

—the glorification of Napoleon, Cesare Borgia, etc.—as self-exaltation. The answer to this is that these types praised by Nietzsche are the exact opposite of himself. But because the opinion of the one is erroneous, that of the other is not on that account correct. The second group recognizes the diversity between the norms and the philosopher's own features; but they do not recognize the intimate bond which unites the two. The truth is that the closest connection exists between the pronounced opposites of these two factors. There are two kinds of philosophic personalities to be distinguished here. In one kind the ethical views are the ideals of one's own actions and feelings. The ideal is the Platonic idea of the author—Spinoza, Kant, Fichte!—or else, the logically developed ideal grows out of one's own being, the dissatisfaction with one's own deeds. Then there arises a dualism, a dividedness—*Zerrissenheit*—in the nature of the preacher of the ideal. The more powerful this nature, all the more glowing is its need of redemption, all the more counter to its own life and being is its ideal;—such is the case with Schopenhauer, Wagner, and Nietzsche. As Nietzsche said: "Our defects are the eyes with which we see the ideal. In both cases the theory of value is intimated, intergrown with the kernel of personality, whether the content of personality be in identity or contrast with that theory of value."

Here, then, is Nietzsche's personality of strength and fineness, of hardness and softness, of delicacy of sentiment and refinement of taste; a personality of storm and calm; a personality of the elegance and good taste and æsthetic qualities of the artist, of the sincerity and truthfulness of the scientist, of the heroism and venturesomeness and tumultuousness of the prophet;—here is this personality revealing itself in every line, in every aphorism. In his own eyes his philosophy was the expression of a personality, of a character, of a temperament.

And surely, we must take this into account, along with his style, when we read what he has to say on war and woman and religion, especially. For example, when Nietzsche cries: "Be hard, O, my brothers, be hard!" what does he mean? "Give your friend a hard bed!" he adjures us. "War and courage have done more great things than love of neighbor has." "Not your sympathy but your bravery rescues the unfortunate."

Nietzsche's head is as hard as iron, like Darwin's; his heart as soft as down, like Schopenhauer's. If the reader relate Nietzsche's hard doctrine to his soft heart, and his tender utterance to his hard head, or make any other adjustment of the matter, he must of course take the consequences in interpretation.

Another question should be raised here, which bears upon our problem along with style and personality, namely,—the antecedents of Nietzsche's hard doctrine. These antecedents begin with the Greek sophists, especially with Kallikles, who in Plato's *Gorgias* developed similar doctrines as to the rights of the stronger. Moral and religious limitations are not "from Nature," but through precept; laws are made only by the weak, the miserable, the many, for the purpose of their protection against the strong. But Nature wills dominion on the part of the strong. According to Nature it is right that the stronger rule over the weaker and that the mightier have an advantage over the less mighty. The more powerful, the stronger, shall rightly, according to natural law, conquer. This sophistic antimorality thus considers moral laws as unnatural fetters, which the strong snap without hesitation, with a good conscience, in order that they may fulfill the will of Nature.

Other phenomena of antiquity may be recalled,—the Cynics, for example. Some baptize Nietzsche's tendency simply as neocynicism. Or, the skeptics (Anaxarchus, teacher of Pyrrho), who accompanied Alexander the Great on his triumphal exploits, and fortified Alexander later to be a Superman and to exercise his right to rise above all restrictions. Or, again, certain phenomena of the Middle Ages may be remembered, especially the Assassins, with whom Nietzsche consciously associated himself. Often Nietzsche adopted their slogan: "Nothing is true, everything is permissible." Again, there were the Renaissance men, among whom Nietzsche sought the exemplar of his Superman—Machiavelli, Agrippa von Nettesheim, Montaigne. Many others see in Thomas Hobbes a forerunner of Nietzsche's *Homo homini lupus*.

Still other exemplars may be found among the *illuminati* of the Eighteenth Century, Mandeville, Marquis de Sade, or even Vauvenargues. Then there is that Frenchman with whom Nietzsche is so often compared—Rousseau, the preacher of a return to nature from the aberrations and the decadence of hyperculture.

In Germany also at that time there was a movement in which one may find parallels to Nietzsche—the period of *Sturm und Drang*—the Genius time with Genius morality, from which the young Goethe did not stand aloof. Reference may be made to a similar phenomenon in the Nineteenth Century—Romanticism, fastening itself to

Fichte's doctrine, finding its typical expression in Schlegel's malodorous novel *Lucinde*.

Finally, Nietzsche is often tied up with Max Stirner, who employed the Hegelian dialectic to ridicule Feuerbach's Humanity philosophy and to replace the abstraction Humanity with the concrete individual ego—all this in his famous book, *Der Einzige und sein Eigenthum,* a book which became the Bible of the so-called "Edel-Anarchisten," with whose leader, Krapotkin, Nietzsche likewise has been associated.

Certainly now, this is a rich and interesting list of forerunners of Nietzsche. In view of such a list we may not dismiss the hardness of Nietzsche, of which his war doctrine is in part expressive, as the storminess of an unbalanced mind. Nietzsche is rather the representative of a tendency which appears from time to time in the history of culture—usually as extreme reaction against an antecedent, one-sided overextension of authority on the part of human society; against the exactions of its culture upon the individual; in short, a *reaction of nature against culture*.

Yet Nietzsche is not to be explained by his kinship with his forerunners simply; he is a thoroughly original nature at the same time. It will be remembered that in his own way Nietzsche made a new synthesis of Schopenhauer and Darwin, transcending each and both of them.

It is against a background of this kind and in the light of these considerations that we should read what Nietzsche says about war. A soft heart could not want war for war's sake, for pain's sake, for death's sake, if peace meant decadence. Always Nietzsche was asking: "What is the cure of decadence? What is an expression and generation of more strength—or what of more weakness?" In such a matter as this, Neitzsche made large ethical use of the Darwinian formula. He points out that among individuals nature tends to kill off the sickly, the less fit, both in body and in mind; nature would preserve the sturdy and robust; these in turn were more likely to beget a race that is physically desirable. What disease and failure did in the life-struggle of individuals, war must do in the conflict of nations. A people, too, might become effete, anæmic, unworthy of its place. It were well for such a people to be dispossessed by a hardier, a more masterful, stock. And to complain of the injustice of such things was to be misled by conventional morality. Would Nietzsche then agree with Bernhardi's notorious aphorism: "The verdict of war is biologically just"? We shall see.

Nietzsche was Darwinian also in his thought of the individual man's career. He conceived the life of man as an heroic battle against all error and illusion. Nature appears to him to be a terrible and often maleficent force. History seems to him "brutal and senseless." The mission of the higher man is to give no quarter to whatever is bad, to dispel all errors, to denounce all false and over-rated values, and to show himself pitiless toward all the weaknesses, all the meannesses, all the lying of civilization. "I dream," he writes in *Ideals of the Future* (Section 8) "of an association of men who will be entire and absolute, who will pay no regard to their conduct or discretion, and will call themselves destroyers; they will submit everything to their criticism, and will sacrifice themselves to truth. Whatever is bad and false must be brought into the light of day! We will not construct before the proper time; we do not know whether we can ever build, or whether it would be better never to build at all. There are lazy pessimists, resigned ones—we shall never be of their number."

Nietzsche's ideal man hates and despises the vulgar worldly prosperity aimed at by the average man; and destroys everything that merits destruction, heedless of his own suffering, heedless of the suffering he causes those about him, borne up in his painful journey through life by his resolute will to be true and sincere at all costs.

The wise man, according to Nietzsche, does not promise men peace and the quiet enjoyment of the fruits of their toil. Nietzsche exhorts men to war—he dazzles their eyes with the hope of victory.

Ye shall seek your enemy [says Zarathustra], ye shall fight your fight, you shall do battle for your thought! And if your thought succumbs, your loyalty must rejoice at its defeat.

Ye shall love peace as a means to new wars, and the short peace more than the long.

I do not counsel you to work, but to fight. I do not counsel peace, but victory. Let your work be a fight; let your peace be a victory.

A good cause, ye say, sanctifies even war; but I say unto you that a good war sanctifies every cause.

For your enemies ye must have hateful adversaries, not contemptible adversaries. Ye must be proud of your enemy, then the successes of your enemy will be also your successes.

In Nietzsche's opinion the open war of rival and contrary forces is the most powerful instrument of progress. Such war shows where there is weakness, where there is physical and moral health, where there is disease. War constitutes one of those dangerous "experiments" undertaken by the wise man to further the progress of life, to test the value of an idea, of a thought, from the point of view of the development of life. Hence war is beneficial, good in itself; and thus Nietzsche predicts without dismay or regret that Europe is not far from entering into a period of great wars when nations will fight with one another for the mastery of the world.

Is Nietzsche then responsible, in his measure, for Prussian militarism, so called, and the recent great war? Without special pleading, I will present the evidence on both sides, and leave the reader to draw his own conclusions.

First: To Nietzsche the term war did not primarily suggest battlefields, but something quite different. He thought of it in the sense in which it was used by Heraclitus, for whom Nietzsche felt the warmest admiration, and whose philosophy suggested to him so much of his own. As a general rule, when Nietzsche speaks of war, he means the interplay of cosmic forces or the opposition to oppressive conventions, or the struggle with one's own passions and impulses to secure self-mastery.

Second: His war doctrine was evolved after the Franco-Prussian war of 1870. In the very hour of German triumph, he was most scathing in his criticism of the tendencies he observed in the Fatherland. Here I wish to make a number of brief quotations from Nietzsche:

Public opinion in Germany seems strictly to forbid any allusion to the evil and dangerous consequences of a war, more particularly when the war in question has been a victorious one. Writers are jubilant in their praise of war, and of the powerful influence war has brought to bear upon morality and culture and art. But of all evil results due to the last contest with France, the most deplorable is that German culture was also victorious in the struggle. This error is in the highest degree pernicious. French culture remains as heretofore, and we Germans depend upon it as heretofore. Our culture did not even help toward the success of our arms. Severe military discipline, natural bravery and sustaining power, the superior generalship, unity and obedience in the rank and file—in short, factors which have nothing to do with culture, were instrumental in making us conquer an opponent in whom the most essential of these factors were absent.

So, in the very hour of Germany's greatest triumph, 1871, Nietzsche dared tell his countrymen that the culture of vanquished France was incomparably superior to theirs. Again and again he denounced German State-idolatry, its militarism, its fanatical patriotism, the Bismarckian worship of success and the arrogant creed of Deutschland: *"Deutschland über alles."*

Again Nietzsche writes: "But nothing shall stop me from being rude and from telling the Germans one or two unpleasant home truths: who else would do it, if I did not? I refer to their laxity in historical matters." Here in caustic terms he denounces the "political puppets" and "tyrannical politicians" who alter and touch up history so that there is constant danger of murder and war. Then Nietzsche turns to Treitschke and exclaims contemptuously: "There is such a thing as writing history according to the lights of Imperial Germany; there is also anti-Semitic history; there is also history written with an eye to *the Court,* and Herr von Treitschke is not ashamed of himself."

Nietzsche asserts also that readiness for war involves the withdrawal, year after year, of "the ablest, strongest, and most industrious men in extraordinary numbers from their proper occupations and callings to be turned into soldiers."

If a nation would count as a Great Power, as we shall see below, it must "constantly sacrifice a number of its most conspicuous talents upon the 'Altar of the Fatherland.'" This meant a "public hecatomb," he said. The individual could no longer live his own life, and one might well ask whether it pays in the end. Nietzsche objects to an excessive preoccupation with military matters in time of peace. Conscriptions may be a good thing as an antidote against decadence, but there are, he thinks, other preventives of decadence which do not entail such a waste of energy.

Moreover, he had his suspicions about the honesty and the wisdom of the doctrine of "Armed Peace." His criticism here is well worth noting.

To one more item I would refer in this connection—Nietzsche's own ideal was not the dominance of any one people, but a cosmopolitan culture. This is attested by his most favorite phrase, "European men." He insists that the day of separate, hostile nationalities is passing, that it has been preserved mainly in the interest of certain royal dynasties, or of social and commercial classes, but that a blending is now to be looked for. In *Human, all-too-Human* he cries: "We should just fearlessly style ourselves 'good Europeans,' and labor actively for the amalgamation of nations."

So much at least may be adduced in support of the thesis that Nietzsche was antimilitaristic. On the other side, there is the following passage in *Human, all-too-Human,* on war as a remedy for national weakness:

For nations that are growing weak and contemptible war may be prescribed as a remedy, if indeed they really want to go on living. National consumption as well as individual admits of a brutal cure. The eternal will to live and inability to die is, however, in itself already a sign of senility of emotion. The more fully and thoroughly we live, the more ready we are to sacrifice life for a single pleasurable emotion. A people that lives and feels in this wise has no need of war.

Again, Nietzsche makes an emphatic pronouncement in favor of war as indispensable:

It is nothing but fanaticism and beautiful-soulism to expect very much (or even, much only) from humanity when it has forgotten how to wage war. For the present, we know of no other means whereby the rough energy of the camp, the deep impersonal hatred, the cold-bloodedness of murder with a good conscience, the general ardor of the system in the destruction of the enemy, the proud indifference to great losses, to one's own existence and that of one's friends, the hollow earthquakelike convulsion of the soul, can be as forcibly and certainly communicated to enervated nations as is done by every great war: owing to the brooks and streams that here break forth, which, certainly, sweep stones and rubbish of all sorts along with them and destroy the meadows of delicate cultures, the mechanism in the workshops of the mind is afterwards, in favorable circumstances, rotated by new power. Culture can by no means dispense with passions, vices, and malignities. When the Romans, after having become imperial, had grown rather tired of war, they attempted to gain new strength by beast-baitings, gladiatorial combats, and Christian persecutions. The English of to-day, who appear on the whole also to have renounced war, adopt other means in order to generate anew those vanishing forces; namely, the dangerous exploring expeditions, sea voyages and mountaineerings, nominally undertaken for scientific purposes, but in reality to bring home surplus strength from adventures and dangers of all kinds. Many other such substitutes for war will be discovered, but perhaps precisely thereby it will become more and more obvious that such a highly cultivated and therefore necessarily enfeebled humanity as that of modern Europe not only needs wars, but the greatest and most terrible wars,—consequently occasional relapses into barbarism,—lest, by the means of culture, it should lose its culture and its very existence.

And finally, touching certain detriments inherent in High Politics, Nietzsche writes:

Just as a nation does not suffer the greatest losses that war and readiness for war involve through the expenses of the war, or the stoppage of trade and traffic, or through the maintenance of a standing army,—however great these losses may now be, when eight European States expend yearly the sum of five milliards of marks thereon,—but owing to the fact that year after year its ablest, strongest, and most industrious men are withdrawn in extraordinary numbers from their proper occupations and callings to be turned into soldiers: in the same way, a nation that sets about practising high politics and securing a decisive voice among the Great Powers does not suffer its greatest losses where they are usually supposed to be. In fact, from this time onward it constantly sacrifices a number of its most conspicuous talents upon the "Altar of the Fatherland" or of national ambition, whilst formerly other spheres of activity were open to those talents which are now swallowed up by politics. But apart from these public hecatombs, and in reality much more horrible, there is a drama which is constantly being performed simultaneously in a hundred thousand acts; every able, industrious, intellectually striving man of a nation that thus covets political laurels, is swayed by this covetousness, and no longer belongs entirely to himself alone, as he did formerly; the new daily questions and cares of the public welfare devour a daily tribute of the intellectual and emotional capital of every citizen; the sum of all these sacrifices and losses of individual energy and labor is so enormous that the political growth of a nation almost necessarily entails an intellectual impoverishment and lassitude, a diminished capacity for the performance of works that require great concentration and specialization. The question may finally be asked: "Does it then *pay,* all this bloom and magnificence of the total (which indeed only manifests itself as the fear of the new Colossus in other nations, and as the compulsory favoring by them of national trade and commerce), when all the nobler, finer, and more intellectual plants and products, in which its soil was hitherto so rich, must be sacrificed to this coarse and opalescent flower of the nation?"

The case is substantially before the reader.

If I may express a personal opinion in closing this paper, it would be this: According to Nietzsche, the best —the aristocratic in that sense—shall rule, and by means of force. In that respect Nietzsche approved of war, but by the term war he usually meant the battle of life. Life was to him an ἀγών, as the Greeks say. We have then, to *train* for the contest. The body which is whole and healthy will possess the *mens sana.* Nietzsche puts it before us that we ought unflinchingly and courageously to take our part in the eternal fight, and to face the struggle like gods. The principle of contest is an essential part of the eternal order, as Nietzsche with his naturalism and evolutionism well knew, and so he held a gladiatorial theory of existence.

CHAPTER SEVEN

Nietzsche and Democracy

In his *Ecce Homo* Nietzsche tells us that with his book, *The Dawn of Day*, "begins my campaign against current morality . . . that the reader should close the book with a rather timid chariness concerning everything that has hitherto been worshiped and honored as 'morality' is not in contradiction to the fact that no negative phrase is to be found in the book, no sudden attack, no malignity. . . ." Perhaps the reason for this unwonted mildness is that *The Dawn of Day* was written at the close of his Intellectualism Period, 1880, when Nietzsche was pushing the idea of sober science to its utmost extreme. For the harshness of his judgments on current values during his third period is without a parallel, unless parts of Heine be excepted; and they have proved offensive to many people. But there was method in Nietzsche's madness, for he knew that his anathemas and blasphemies were necessary weapons in the kind of warfare he had to wage.

But as to this *The Dawn of Day*, his sister tells us that during its preparation he devoted a great deal of his time and attention to the study of political questions, particularly socialism:

In *The Dawn of Day* he expressed as favorable an opinion as possible on such subjects. At the same time he adheres firmly to his earlier formula, that the worth of a nation—indeed of all mankind—is seen in its highest specimens of men. Despite his personal goodwill, therefore, my brother had perforce to be an enemy of socialism, especially of its leaders, not only on account of the ignobleness of their sentiments and aims, which are in opposition to everything mighty, beautiful, and cultured; but also because, as he threw in their teeth, they made the masses discontented and unhappy; they aroused their eagerness for conditions, and consoled them with hopes which were neither desirable nor attainable.

So his sister explains, perhaps I should say, mitigates his attitude.

Then comes Peter Gast, a lifelong friend, with his explanation:

Nietzsche [he says], saw in democracy a clear sign of degeneration, and, above all, of want of noble feelings and of conspicuous and directing master minds; and it was his opinion that the design of correcting and improving the human race by beginning with men of the third and fourth order (instead of at the top), or of leading to a higher level by the emancipation of woman, was the most baleful aberration of judgment it was possible to conceive.

With these biographical references, we may turn from Nietzsche to Nietzsche's doctrine. Perhaps it should be said that, for Nietzsche, Democracy, Socialism, Anarchism, with superficial differences, are to be classed together, and, along with Christianity, their root and womb, are to be condemned as at once cause and effect of modern degeneracy, mediocrity, and vulgarity. By way of procedure I shall first give a brief summary treatment of the subject; then, secondly, unfold the aspects of the theme at once more comprehensively and more minutely; and, thirdly, appraise the net results, with a word of criticism and appreciation.

First, then, what is the important point as to social democracy? It is well known that from the point of view of the current morality of "peace on earth, goodwill toward men," Nietzsche came to be an antimoralist, or, if the reader will, an amoralist. He did not hold to the traditional distinction between good and evil. To the anti-natural morality of the "weak," he opposed the natural morality of the "strong."

This, of course, is well known; but it is not so well known that this antimoralistic tendency is only a small section of Nietzsche's total doctrine. Nietzsche really shows a characteristic many-sidedness of nature, or, to use a word that he likes, *Vielsaitigkeit,* "a harp of a thousand strings." He is a polyphone nature, specializing in tonicity.

Now, Nietzsche's antisocialistic tendency is closely akin to his antimoralism. He is a spirited foe to all binding of the individual on the part of society and State. Socialists strive, he thinks, for the socializing of all functions, to the point of abrogating individual autonomy and initiative, with the view of safeguarding the people from exploitation by overmastering individuals. As against this position, Nietzsche preaches that the salvation of *Kultur* reposes only on individuals, to whom the masses are ministrant. Men are either one or the other of two things, rulers or ruled. There is need of master-men by nature, of men who impose their will upon others. That is, Nietzsche sees the salvation of humanity, not in the masses, but only in strong individuals, in natures who have energetic, self-conscious personalities. But a personality has a stamp of its own, whose sharp lines are not spent or washed out. It is one of Nietzsche's deepest convictions that such great individuals do not grow—cannot grow—in a socialistic society, or, indeed, in a State, that is, the present State, with its numberless laws, which abridge the individual and retard the unfolding of great individualities. Thus his antisocialistic tendency takes on ultimately in this sense an antipolitical tendency even to the extreme of anarchistic individualism. This, however, is not democracy. He is the strongest opponent of all democracy—a remark which must be modified, certainly explained, later. Nietzsche is a most ardent champion of aristocracy. The corollate to this is his antidemocratic tendency. He calls the masses *die Viel-zu-Vielen,* one of his best known watchwords. To Nietzsche the masses are only cannon fodder in the struggle for existence, only a foil for setting off to advantage the few betters; but the betters are the stronger, who rightfully rule on that account and oppress the weak. This aristocratic tendency ties up intimately with Niezsche's faith in the perfectible power of the struggle for existence. Life is a war of all living beings against one another, and in this *bellum omnium contra omnes,* the stronger triumph, the privileges of strength are increased. In this sense, nature itself is an aristocratic institution. Nietzsche simply transfers this aristocracy of nature to the history of *Kultur* and to cultural relationships; the right of the stronger is to him the right which nature herself wills.

All this is less offensive than it seems, as later discussion will bring out. Meantime we are now concerned with the deduction of these affirmations of Nietzsche from his basic principle—namely, his Will to Power, in connection with the Darwinian "struggle for existence" and "natural selection." Nietzsche assumes these two laws, and agrees that democracy and socialism, like Christianity, oppose these laws; that by this opposition the race is weakened, since it detracts from the power of the individual and consequently lessens his chance for existence. He makes a plea for the adoption of standards compatible with the laws of existence,—or, better, not of existence, but of progress, ascent, fulness of life. He points out that the race has been on the decline for centuries, has been almost irremediably weakened by adherence to democratic, socialistic, Christian, antinatural doctrines; and that each day of such activity is another step in the degeneration of man.

Now it seems to me that with Nietzsche's ground principle in mind, with this kernel and root laid bare, we can understand all the tendencies of his thinking. For instance, do Democrats and Socialists deplore the strain and pain and suffering of life, as he says they do? But if the victory of the stronger over the weaker is willed by nature; if nature really needs the struggle for existence in order to improve the species, then may we complain about the fact of struggle and evil? If we will the *end*, the perfecting of the species, the elevation and higher formation of life, must we not also will the *means*, the struggle of the will-centers among themselves, the victory of the stronger, the downfall of the weaker? Especially must we not affirm, approve, even will, all cruelty which is necessarily bound up with the struggle? To bemoan and lament this cruelty of the war of life is a miserable, unmanly weakness and antinaturalness; it is a nihilistic decadence. We should say *yes* to life; we should love fate, even the hardest fate. *Amor fati*—there is the whole of Nietzsche's soul. All whining is miserable slave-weakness, and rests on coddling and pampering. Heroic natures, master-natures,—these do not whine; they fight away with laughter on their lips; falling, they still laugh. Of course, conflict and war mean numberless and bitter woes; but the sound will affirms this woe of the struggle for existence in every particular as necessary means to the elevation of the level of life. In one word, without struggle, no progress; without pain, no struggle. Woe strengthens the strong, weakens the weak. Woe's vocation and function are thus fulfilled; that the weak fall and the strong rise higher and higher.

Once man counted the evil of the world as a disproof of God. So, Leibnitz, for example, wrote a *théodicée, i.e.,* a justification of God, arguing that this was the best possible world because there was more pleasure than pain, because there were more homes than hospitals. For *théodicée* Nietzsche writes *cosmodicée, physiodicée, biodicé.* He justifies, not God, as the Church counts God; for Nietzsche's God is the universe in the course of its evolution, becoming God whenever it arrives at the stage of maximum power; then ceasing to be God as it begins its course of declining or descending life, until it passes from its nadir to its zenith again, and so on incessantly. In his *The Will to Power,* Nietzsche says: "God is the culminating moment; life is an eternal process of deifying and undeifying." If you think of the universe as a clock, it is God always when it strikes twelve noon! But Nietzsche does not justify God; he justifies the world, nature, life. It is from this standpoint that he works with a view to the joy of existence, that is, the joy of the game, of the fight. *"Mensch sein, heisst ein Kämpfer sein,"* Goethe had already said. Nietzsche adds: Man should fight joyously, not merely courageously. In the steel bath of this war-joy, this life-joy, our sick time can find convalescence; our pessimistic, pathological decadent *Zeitgeist* can become sound again.

Such is the soul of Nietzsche. *The natural instincts of life are positive*. Negative asceticism is to be rejected. Positive asceticism, that is, the resolute habituation to pain for the sake of life, for the sake of power, is to be affirmed. From the very bottom up life is pleasure, in spite of pain. Even pain itself is a wellspring of pleasure to the sound man, the strong man, because in war upon pain he realizes, effectuates, his will, his original instincts, more and more. It is only in the light of this joy of existence, in spite of all the woe of existence,—this war-glad, overflowing, superabounding joy of even the *Amor fati,* that we can understand Nietzsche's attitude toward democracy.

Take Nietzsche's thought of the root of democracy and socialism—the religious root. Schopenhauer did not occupy so unfriendly an attitude to Christianity as many seem to think. Indeed, no other modern philosopher penetrated so profoundly as did he into the essence of Christianity, so warmly defended the kernel of Christianity. More friendly is he to it than its much lauded champions, such as Kant, Fichte, Schelling, Hegel, Herbart, even Schleiermacher. Schopenhauer especially praised three Christian thoughts, evil, love, and contempt of the world. Physical and moral evil plays a big rôle with Schopenhauer. He understood Christianity on that point rather thoroughly. Love recurs in Schopenhauer as pity, the universal principle of morals for him. World-contempt, world-flight, first found in Schopenhauer its philosophical explanation and justification. Monasticism, asceticism, virginity,—never was praise of them better than Schopenhauer's, nor practice of them worse! One could distill a striking apologetic for Christianity from Schopenhauer.

But we could expect no such apologetic attitude from Nietzsche! It was precisely that *positive turn* which he took under the influence of Darwinism and the Schopenhauerian doctrine of the will which conditioned his negative attitude toward Christianity and, consequently, democracy. Christian pessimism was offensive to him, particularly its basic concept of moral evil, of sin. He thought that this sin concept destroyed the freshness of life, the joy of life. Priests were falsifiers of the values of life, as they were falsifiers of conscience. Priests called the natural, the instinctive, the original,—"sin"! Cowardice, impuissance, bloodlessness; priests called these "virtues." They substituted their pale virtue for blooming and blossoming life; they scorned the life of the body, degraded the body to a bloodless shadow. This whole Christian pessimistic conception of life and of man Nitzsche repudiated.

He dealt likewise with the second concept, love. Love is *pity;*—but life is *pitilessness*. Life is wrestling and warring, *Sturm und Drang*. These promote life; pity retards life. Wrestling and warring weed out life's incompetents, preserve only life's competent ones. Pity is anti-natural.

And so is the third concept, contempt of the world, flight from the world. This concept is an ingratitude to nature, whose children we are. Nature has destined us to be warriors and workers; Christianity would rob us of the joy of war and the lust of work. We are to labor on the world, and on ourselves, to give meaning to the world. Christianity rejects this world as world, as worldly, and yearns for an invented, imaginary hereafter, leading us to neglect our duty to nature and life. Christianity makes us slaves of a fictitious God, instead of masters of this real world. Nietzsche fought, therefore, with unparalleled bitterness against Christianity. And, of course, if he is right in his basic principle, he is right in his fight.

Now, it is from this principle and this Christianity that we are to understand his reactions to socialism, democracy, and anarchy. "Anarchy and Christianity sprang from the same womb," he says in *Anti-Christ;* "Anarchists are at one with the socialists," he explains in *Beyond Good and Evil;* "An agitatory measure of socialism," he declares in *The Will to Power*. Again, "Anarchy is a result of decadence. The Christian and the anarchist are both decadents," he shows. Democrats, socialists, anarchists,—these are all fundamentally the same thing to Nietzsche, are all born of weakness, all breed weakness, are all Christians at bottom.

But we are concerned with democracy first. It is unnecessary to observe that Darwinism is a doctrine of Aristocracy. According to Darwinism, it is a law of life that the stronger triumph over the weaker in the struggle for existence. Darwinism teaches the increase of privilege, of advantage, precisely through this struggle of existence, as well as through hereditation: pure aristocratic traits. Also, for Nietzsche, it is the economy willed by nature that the stronger should attain to dominion. Those individuals in whom not simply the will to live but the Will to Power is most vital rightly come to the fore; the natural principle realizes itself in them most completely, and they hereditarily pass on their excellences to their successors. Here is explained Nietzsche's fanatical praise for the old aristocratic France of the Seventeenth and Eightenth centuries, for its privileges, its exclusiveness, the fineness and loftiness of its culture. Occasionally Nietzsche seems an enthusiastic admirer of the nobility of Poland. This proclivity brought him many disciples, such as they were.

It so happens that this aristocracy *schämerei* of Nietzsche fell in harmoniously with a tendency of his day. The might of the nobility was on the increase in Germany. But his aristocracy took on a different aspect when he faced forward to the future. Facing forward, there was nothing of that hereditary aristocracy reposing on frequently doubtful birth! He speaks of breeding future men. He speaks of the aristocracy, not of birth, not of wealth, not of rank; but of the *aristocracy of will,* which can develop everywhere where man meets man. It is to these aristocratic spirits in general to which Nietzsche turns in opposition to the *Viel-zu-Vielen.* And it is for these aristocratic spirits that Nietzsche creates a new table of values, a code of exclusiveness and of refinement which separates them entirely as superiors from the masses who moil and toil. Artists and authors, scholars, too, leading spirits in all regions: they feel that they have the right to count themselves members of the aristocracy. But what is the slogan of democracy, so fascinating to the rabble? "Equal rights for all!"—a leveling, flattering thing! Equality before God, so it begins!—then equality before nature; equality before the law; equality before morality; and finally equality before opportunity. It is all false! cries Nietzsche, false from top to bottom! Not equality of all, but inequality of all! And just because men are so unequal in will and worth, Nietzsche hates the *Gleichmacherei* of democracy; Nietzsche sees in it a wrong against nature, which has created men unequally. Nature itself has propounded to us the "problem of the order of rank." We sin against nature when we inaugurate an artificial equality where nature has evoked in her wisdom an inequality. And this inequality of kind must carry with it inequality of right. The superior, the powerful, the energetic, are born to rule; the mass of the inferior, the weak, the will-less, are to be ruled, and the rulers must keep them at the necessary "distance of dependence." But if the masses take the reins into their own hands, then the superior and the noble draw back instinctively. Nietzsche finds the vocation of the masses to serve as a sort of pedestal for the few aristocratic spirits. Here his watchword of the *Viel-zu-Vielen* matches Schopenhauer's watchword of the *Dutzendware der Natur* (odds and ends of nature). But Schopenhauer softens this haughty expression by his pity morality. Nietzsche, however, has gone through the hard school of Darwinism and its struggle doctrine, and knows not this "pity" mitigation. *Kultur* should be as pitiless and unmerciful as nature herself. The *Viel-zu-Vielen* serve only as footstools for the few select and exceptional men.

And Nietzsche ties up socialism with democracy. Socialism subordinates the individual to society as a ministrant member thereof and equalizes him with all others. Socialism places the weal of society, of the masses, of the majority, above the wishes and aims of the individual. It represses individuality for the sake of society. Nothing could be more anti-Nietzschean than this. Where could there be any Will to Power in a socialistic society? The individual would there be condemned to powerlessness; the individual would there be repressed; acquisitive struggles for outstanding positions of power would cease, or at least be falsified. Everything would then be regulated, ordered, leveled, made mediocre. The individual would be robbed of his power. At best, in place of free, open power, there would be secret cunning and base intrigue. But all chivalrous, knightly energy would be gone. Socialism would replace the rough struggle of existence with social peace, "the piping times of peace." Socialism protects the weak against the overpower of the strong. Socialism makes the weak stronger, the strong weaker. How inevitable it was that this teacher of inequality should hate the equalizing tendency of socialism. Nietzsche saw that our age is becoming more and more collectivistic, and that therefore it is forgetting to honor the basic right, the basic worth of the individual. He warned against the omnipotence of society, of State, of bureaucracy. The bearers and leaders of *Kultur* are great personalities—to whom our democratic, socialistic, bureaucratic time is an implacable foe. Magnify society, minify individuality—that is the way, thought Nietzsche, to the ruin of the race.

We may fittingly conclude this chapter with the following passages from Nietzsche:

For the mediocre, it is a joy to be mediocre. . . . It would be absolutely unworthy of a profound thinker to see any objective to mediocrity *per se*. For, in itself, it is the first condition under which exceptions are possible, and a high culture is determined by it. [According to Nietzsche, then, the mediocre may live happy and useful lives in their own way.]

FRIEDRICH NIETZSCHE

[From this arises Nietzsche's fury against socialists.] Whom do I hate most among all the rabble of to-day? The socialist, who undermines the working-man's instincts, who destroys his satisfaction with his insignificant existence, who makes him envious and teaches him revenge.

And what is freedom? The will to be responsible for one's self. The will to keep that distance which separates man from man. The will to become indifferent to hardship, severity, privation, and even to life. The will to sacrifice men, and even one's own cause, and to sacrifice one's self, too. . . . The man who is truly free tramples under foot the contemptible species of well-being dreamt of by shopkeepers, Christians, cows, women, Englishmen, and other democrats. The free man is a warrior. . . . How is freedom to be measured? By the resistance it has to overcome, by the effort required to maintain it.

I do not advise you to labor but to fight. I do not advise you to compromise and make peace, but to conquer. Let your labor be fighting and your peace be victory. . . . You say that a good cause will hallow even war? I tell you that a good war hallows every cause. War and courage have done more great things than charity. Not your pity, but your bravery lifts up those about you. Let sentimental women tell you that "good" means "sweet and touching." I tell you that "good" means "brave." . . . The slave rebels against hardship and calls his rebellion superiority. Let your superiority be an acceptance of hardships. Let your commanding be an obeying. . . . Let your highest thought be: Man is something to be surpassed.

I do not advise you to love your neighbor—your nearest human being. I advise you to flee from the nearest and love the farthest human being. Higher than love to your neighbor is love to the highest man that is to come in the future. . . . Propagate yourself upward. Thus live your life. What are many years worth? I do not spare you. . . . Die at the right time!

CHAPTER EIGHT

Nietzsche and Science

THE subject of this chapter is Nietzsche and Science, but a fuller designation would be Nietzsche and Intellectualism. What precisely is meant by intellectualism will appear later.

For this time one brief biographical mention must suffice. It is the influence upon Nietzsche of Dr. Paul Rée—an influence exaggerated by Frau Salomé in her book to which I have referred. Still it is undeniable that Rée was to some extent responsible for Nietzsche's philosophical transition from his first period to his second; that is, toward intellectualism, or empiricism, or, if the reader will, science. Rée and Nietzsche were both interested in the French aphoristic writers, such as La Rochefoucauld, La Bruyère, Fontenelle, Vauvenargues, and Chamfort, and in the French philosophical writers, such as Voltaire, Pascal, and Stendhal. But it must be especially noted that in all probability it was Rée's own book, *The Origin of the Moral Feelings,* that led Nietzsche into the camp of the English positivists, Darwin, Spencer, John Stuart Mill, and others. Indeed, in a letter to Rée, Nietzsche says: "The English philosophical writers furnish the only good philosophical intercourse now."

But does the term "transition" sum up the life of Nietzsche? Yes and no. Yes. "All things flow like a stream," said Tennyson. Nietzsche, as the holder of a similar doctrine, was a modern Heraclitus. As a true teacher of "the flux," Nietzsche underwent constant changes, and if one ties up a doctrine of his with the wrong point in the flux, his meaning is lost, and things are hopelessly tangled. His mind was a flux; and his enemies pretend that, had he lived a few more years, he himself would have overthrown his "eternal" philosophy.

Constant transition—yes! But, for all that, there was something that did *not* change, to lose sight of which, as is so often done by Nietzsche's interpreters, is to misunderstand him, and misrepresent him even. Through all his changes Nietzsche is the philosopher of *Kultur,* and seeks to organize a *hierarchy of values. Kultur* is the problem to which all his most essential thoughts are related. This problem is not affected by the alteration and alternation of his views. *Kultur,* the worth-problem, unites the periods of his thought, and stands central in his philosophy. First, *Kultur* is *art,* "the unity," he says in *The Birth of Tragedy,* "of the artistic style in all the manifestations of a people's life." Secondly, *Kultur* is *knowledge* (*Erkenntnis*); and, in the third period, the goal of *Kultur* is "the *elevation* of the type man." But Nietzsche was not simply a thinker; he was a passionate thinker. He was not satisfied to make the object of his investigation the mere conditions under which *Kultur* arises. From the very beginning, with but little fluctuation, he held it to be the peculiar vocation of the philosopher to create *Kultur,* to set up a new *Kultur* ideal, to summon it into life; that was the goal of his philosophy, and, as he thought, of all genuine philosophy. The task of the philosopher requires that "he create values," he says. "The philosopher uses the will to existence with a view to a higher form of existence." How far are things unchangeable? To that extent, let them alone! But how far are they changeable? One of Nietzsche's most important and fruitful thoughts answers that question: "With the most regardless bravery," he says, "abandon yourself to the improvement of the sides of the world recognized as changeable." Nietzsche's religion—for like every other man he had a religion—was *faith in the improvability of the world*.

In this spirit, then, he sought to discover what contribution science makes to *Kultur*, to worth-creating, to that interest which was the constant throughout the change from period to period of his thinking. The point is not that Nietzsche was a scientific specialist in some field of inquiry. He was at the outset a brilliant philologist (though he gave up philology for a reason which points to his final attitude to science), he had no mean insight into biology, and especially he grubbed and delved into the psychical life of man with an uncanny and demonic insight and skill. But let it be conceded that he was not a scientist in any special field, that he made no contribution to scientific method,—though it is somewhat too generous to grant so much. The point is, nevertheless, that he was the *critic* of science, its evaluator and appraiser. Consequently, his question was: What is the *worth* of science; what is its value in the hierarchy of values? It is exactly the same question which he asked with reference to the State, to morality, to art, to Christianity. And barring a certain bitterness and brutality of speech,—but barring it not much,—he arrived in the end at the *same damnatory judgment* in his appraisal of science that he did in his appraisal of Christianity, and *precisely for the same reason*. Time was when apologists said that Christianity was all and science nothing. "What has Jerusalem to do with Athens?" cried Tertullian. Then apologists agreed that science was of value as well as Christianity, and set about framing a concordat between the two, holding, however, the superior worth of Christianity. Finally, primacy was accorded to science, and Christianity was allowed to exist by courtesy, provided that science could make room for Christianity. Then comes Nietzsche, and launches thunderbolts at both Christianity and science, on the grounds that both are foes to life, to the beauty and power and plenitude of life; that both spring from weakness and make weak, and not from strength and do not make strong. The reader will find I think that if Nietzsche's argument against Christianity is valid, it is equally valid against science. But we are here concerned with Nietzsche's own question, namely, what is the worth of science, and with the answers which he gave in each of his three periods.

If reiteration will not be superfluous here,—it will be worth while to look at those three periods yet once again, but from a different angle of vision. Our task now is to articulate Nietzsche's appraisal of science in what the Germans would call the *Entwicklungsgang* of his soul, of his thought. So, only, can we understand both his intellectualism and, especially, his *anti-intellectualism*.

For the first period a moment will suffice,—period that has been catalogued by Nietzsche's students now as the Æsthetic Period, now as the First Period of the Metaphysician Nietzsche, now as the Metaphysic-Æsthetic-Dionysian Period, now as the Pessimistic Period. Let us call it simply the Art Period, for short. It is the period in which Nietzsche marches under the banner of the Schopenhauer-Wagner view of the world and judgment of life, a period of uncritical enthusiasm, according to which art and music were to redeem the world from misery, an uncritical pessimistic metaphysics, in which the problem of the worth of science does not emerge, although the period is anti-intellectualistic. Nietzsche is now against optimism and rationalism. This first period did not last long, for he soon moved toward a critical enthusiasm, toward the positivistic, the intellectualistic, in which he glorified the scientific man. Now he writes *Human, all-too-Human* in all its four parts, especially *The Wanderer and his Shadow,* and part of *The Dawn of Day.* In these writings the ideal of the artist is replaced by that of the scientist. Only in experience and its employment through the understanding, with the exclusion of all metaphysics, on the one hand, and of the unquiet, impulsive life, on the other,—that is, then, only the empirical understanding, only in and through this, this intellect and knowledge and science, only in experience so understood can passionate man find satisfaction. In particular the Schopenhauerian metaphysics of the will must be renounced. So that Nietzsche is now empiricist, intellectualist, rationalist. The victory of the intellect is the victory of the good. Therefore, Nietzsche is now optimist also. Pessimism goes with the metaphysics of the will.

But Nietzsche is a bird of passage. On he goes into his third and final stage, but back, with important modifications, to Schopenhauer and his doctrine of the will; yet not to art as the redeemer from the will's slavery and misery. He surrenders the intellectualism of the second period, but keeps its optimism. In the third period, the will is not will to live, blind, unhappy, needing redemption, but Will to Power, glad of life, fresh, unbroken. Life is might, the use of might. Life reposes in the instinct to be mighty, to exercise might. This Will to Power is the instinctive basic impulse of all being. But if man, then, too, is fundamentally Will to Power, then the intellect must be assigned second rank. The will is primary, the intellect secondary. So said Schopenhauer, too. But Schopenhauer saw in the intellect, hence in science, in part, a sedative for the unrest of the restless will. This Nietzsche did not say. In the outgrowth of the intellect, in the intellect's stifling of the will, Nietzsche sees the reason for the decadence of man. Precisely where the intellect mounts above the will, the ax is also laid at the root of the will; the will is weakened, energy paralyzed, natural instinct falsified. This original power and energy in the struggle for existence, Nietzsche drew from Darwin. It was on the basis of this Darwinian principle that Nietzsche turned positively now to Schopenhauer again. Thus the striking feature of anti-intellectualism is to be accounted for, without straining a point, on the basic principle of Nietzsche's philosophy. It came about that Nietzsche, a man of the finest intellectual culture, could wage war against the dominion of the intellect, against the overappreciation of intellectual culture. In intellect, he sees *"Die Kleine Vernuft"* of man; *"Die Grosse Vernunft"* of man,—this is the will with its instincts and impulses, in which and out of which the wisdom of nature herself speaks. The origin and spread of *Kultur* is everywhere ascribed to strong-willed personalities; the decline of *Kultur* begins where enlightenment weakens the original will. This was especially true in Greece, with the advent of Socrates, against whom Nietzsche battles as the representative of the hypertrophy of the intellect as compared with the originality of the will. To Nietzsche, Socrates, so praised in the second Science Period, is now the type of the dry scholars who, through their rational dialectics, dessicate, dry up the will. And, as must be shortly shown, it is to be understood in this sense when Nietzsche turns against scholars, against science even, when ultimately he even mocks and derides the very search for truth itself. From the standpoint of Schopenhauer, all intellectual activity is only *Vorstellung,* in the sense that all products of the intellect are only of the nature of ideas, that is, have only a phenomenal character. For Schopenhauer the whole world is only *Vorstellung,* only *trügerischen Schein* (deceptive appearance). Consistently, therefore, for Nietzsche there is no "truth" any more in the old sense. The deceptive ideas of the intellect, however, are not all of equal worth, or rather of equal worthlessness. Here the Darwinian standpoint comes as a corrective among those *Scheinvorstellungen,* those delusion ideas, some of which are life-advancing, while others are life-retarding. A process of natural selection goes on among these delusion ideas; those remain and survive which advance life; the others go down. *Such life-advancing illusions men call truth!* Here is the point where Nietzsche's anti-intellectualism climbs to a mighty transvaluation of every previous concept of truth. Furthermore, the concept of truth, which seems independent of the influence of the will, is now placed in the service of the will to live; the concept of appearance, of illusion, loses its negative sense and gets a positive character as means to life, as organ of the will, as instrument of power.

Such, then, is the anti-intellectualism of Nietzsche's third period, as against the intellectualism of his second period.

In the second period Nietzsche said: *"Fiat veritas, pereat vita!"* In the third period he reversed that saying: *"Fiat vita, pereat veritas!"* "Life is for the sake of truth," he said in the second period, but in the third period, "Truth is for the sake of life."

Now if we declare that "life is for truth," what is the test or criterion of the truth of an idea or belief? The answer is that there is none and can be none. If we say "truth is for the sake of life," then what is the test or criterion of the truth of an idea? The answer is that it serves life, augments the beauty and plenitude and power and productivity of life. A so-called error, or illusion, which thus serves and advances life, is "truer" than a so-called truth which weakens and retards life, just as a so-called wrong which makes life vigorous is better than a so-called right that makes life weak. The question is: Has life been helped by so-called truth more than it has by so-called error? Which has contributed more to life, verity or illusion? Has the intellect's science energized, or tended to paralyze, the will's instincts, impulses, and power? From the standpoint of the Will to Power, is science a will-weakener or a will-strengthener? That is Nietzsche's extraordinary question, and it receives an extraordinary answer.

But we are anticipating. Still, without serious prejudice to my task, I think we may leave the first period to one side, the period in which Nietzsche cherished an *uncriti-*

cal pessimistic voluntarism, and cured life's hurt with *art.* We shall then be concerned with his appraisal of science in the second period, a period of *semi-critical, evolutionistic intellectualism,* labeled now the Intellectual Period, now the Period of the Positivist Nietzsche, now the Æsthetic-Critical-Apollonian Period, now simply the Rationalistic Period. It comprises the years 1876-1883, and the books from *Human, all-too-Human* to *Joyful Wisdom.* With this second period we shall now have to deal; and with the third, also, the period, to use a comprehensive designation again,—the period of a *critical optimistic, evolutionistic voluntarism.* This period has been defined, now as the Ethical Period; now, as the Second Period of the Metaphysical Nietzsche; now as the Physiologic-Æsthetic-Neo-Dionysian Period; now as the Optimistic Period. It comprises the years 1883-1888, and the books from *Zarathustra* to *The Will to Power,* the second volume of Nietzsche's *Will to Power* being his most important work.

In the light of the second and third period, we might phrase our present discussion: Intellectualism or Voluntarism—Which? Or, should a man live for truth, or should he live for life? Is the ideal of science, like that of Christianity,—ascetic? The slogan of science is: *Fiat veritas, pereat vita!* Then is there a virtue more dangerous to life than scientific righteousness? The more knowledge, the less will and feeling? Science—does it not produce walking encyclopedias, bloodless scholars, university professors who no longer feel *immediately,* men incapable of action?

Again we are anticipating, and must come quickly back to the second period of Nietzsche's intellectualism.

After having renounced the guidance of Wagner and turned away from his philosophy and that of Schopenhauer, and after the mists of metaphysical fancies had been swept away by breezes which came to him suddenly from the land of Guyau and from the land of Spencer, Nietzsche became a positivist. Truth was now to be loved, even if its embrace meant death; and Nietzsche now shows his greatest lucidity and his nearest approach to scholarly methods. From Wagner to Darwin, from Schopenhauer to Dr. Paul Rée, a physician, from Heraclitus to Socrates, from Bacchus to Apollo,—wherever was there such a philosophic pilgrimage before? It is perhaps the longest and most hazardous path a philosopher ever trod—this, from uncritical toward critical enthusiasm, from romanticism to a positivism hostile to romanticism. It is a new Nietzsche that now confronts us. What does he have to say? That metaphysics must be excluded from the circle of true philosophy. There is no "thing-in-itself" to be subject-matter of metaphysics. Besides, the psychological motives which have hitherto impelled to metaphysics have not been truth-promoting, nor indifferent to truth, but entirely truth-falsifying. Metaphysics is a product, not of the desire for truth, but of love and of hate, of most personal sympathies, of the need of consolation, of the accidental experiences of life; in short, of all possible feelings and passions, which have nothing to do with truth as such. Nietzsche now says that metaphysics is the science "which treats of the basic errors of man, yet as if they were basic truths." Art, religion, *Kultur* morals, must be taken away from metaphysics and given to anti-metaphysical philosophy. And the method of this philosophy is not to be speculative or artistic, like metaphysics, but a method distinguished in no particular from the scientific.

And the philosopher must eschew anthropomorphism —that is, the projecting of æsthetic, moral, religious, in a word, *Human-all-too-Human,* ideas into things. They are not there; why put them there? Human properties, human points of view, human values are all products of a complicated development and are not to be applied to the elements and foundations of all development from which they grew; they are to be considered as Human-all-too-Human. Schopenhauer's question as to the worth of the world, as to cosmological optimism or pessimism, belongs to unjustifiable and therefore unanswerable questions. Thus philosophy is now resolved into pure science, and previous philosophers, with their personal posing of the problem, are only sorry degenerates of the scientific man. Scientific philosophy must be applied with the scientific method, to religion, art, *Kultur,* and ethics!

But what becomes of those later at the hands of science? Take religion—for what is true of it is true of all the others. For metaphysics religion is a child of transcendent relations. Even in the first period, religion could lay no claim to be true, to have the worth of objective truth. But science places this untruth in a far more glaring light through the discovery of the psychological wellsprings from which religious ideas stream forth. Thus philosophy of religion becomes psychology of religion. Thus it is shown that religion not only speaks of things of which no man can know, but speaks of things on grounds and in a manner and method which are to be referred to demonstrable and knowable errors concerning earthly relations. Thus the truth of religion is undermined. Or shall one retreat to the position that religion as the doctrine of that which is above and beyond experience, moves in a region whose night no human eye can pierce, a region whose door is thrown open, if not to knowledge at least to faith? Religion passes muster on the grounds that the irrepressible needs of the heart impel to definite assumptions concerning that obscure kingdom as to whose truth one can know nothing, but as to whose untruth one can know nothing as well? To believe in religion as something super-rational is therefore allowed. But science comes forward and shows that these definite assumptions repose in gross illusions concerning clearly knowable things lying in the region of experience; and, thus, the night of the super-experiential is no longer able to throw its protecting veil over this now antirational faith and its assumptions. For the source of the error lies no longer in an asylum of ignorance, in the Beyond, but in *the Here and the Now*. Nothing can escape the judgment-seat of science. This is the philosophical sense of the Nietzschean thesis, *viz.*, "There never has been a religion, that, mediately or immediately, as dogma or as parable, has contained a truth. For every religion is born out of anxiety and need, has slipped into existence in the maze of reason." The phenomenon of ascetic sanctity, for example, is to be understood neither as religious miracle of an act of grace (Christianity), nor as a metaphysical miracle of the abrogation of the will (Schopenhauer), but as the complicated interplay of motives of refined vanity, lust of emotions, perverse sexuality, etc. The faith-strong might of such men reposes on an error, namely,—the false interpretation of their states through their interpreters!

[128]

Or, take the demon of Socrates, for which in his *Birth of Tragedy* Nietzsche has sought an all too profound metaphysical explanation, but which in *Human, all-too-Human,* he elucidates by reference to an affection of the ear.

But the most important psychological analysis of this kind is his great examination of *the need of redemption,* out of which the Christian and Buddhistic religions have grown for the most part. This need is referred to a depressing dissatisfaction with one's self and of pain over the imperfection of the world, feelings which Nietzsche seeks to show as the inevitable emotional precipitate of a warped and erroneous judgment concerning one's self and the world. The sum of his argument is that "a definite false psychology, a certain kind of *Phantastik,* in the interpretation of motives and experiences, is the necessary presupposition of one's becoming a Christian and feeling the need of redemption. With insight into this aberration of the reason one ceases to be a Christian."

What, then, has science thus done to the religious life? The explanation of religion is the destruction of religion. Science reduces the theological to the metaphysical, the metaphysical to the psychological, the psychological to the physiological, the chemical, and the physical, and the latter to some sort of mechanics of motion. But what is then true of religion is true of art, of *Kultur,* of morality. These undergo a like reduction, depotentiation, impoverishment, leveling, uniformizing, mechanizing. All these, as known in experience, share precisely the same fate as religion at the hands of science.

This is the truth of science, but is it the life? Does science make life beautiful, abounding, powerful, or does it impoverish life, evacuate it of its content? If the ascetic ideal seeks an essential reduction, privation, negation, of life's instinctive, original, fontal fulness, then does not science come under the head of asceticism along with Christianity and Buddhism and pessimism? Does not the scientific specialist spending his days on a tropical bug, reduce and narrow his own life, like a day laborer, who spends his years making pin heads?

No wonder that sad Nietzsche closed his second period of intellectualism by quoting Byron's *Manfred:*

> Sorrow is knowledge: they who know the most
> Must mourn the deepest o'er the fatal truth:
> The Tree of Knowledge is not that of life!

The real worth-man is the knowledge-man, says Nietzsche's intellectualism, but quick as a flash, he passed at the acme of his intellectualism to the conclusion of the worthlessness of life. His period of enlightenment was his period of gloom, his *Dunkelzeit.* According to his beautiful parable borrowed from a northern winter's day, "the sun of the human future" had temporarily vanished for him.

"Zu viel klarte sich mir auf, nun geht es mich nichts mehr an" (I am too much enlightened, nothing amounts to anything any more). Have I still a *goal,* a haven to which my ship sails? What is left for me? A heart, weary and brazen; an unsteady will, *Flatter-Flügel* (wing-flapping); a broken backbone. Thy danger is no small one, thou free spirit and wanderer! Thou hast lost thy goal, therewith thou hast also lost thy way."

Kultur of the intellect, which is called *Auflärung,* is negative in its effect, it makes man free and "of age," but it does not help him to know the whither of his freedom. Back then to Nietzsche's youthful statement: "It has been shown to be impossible to build *Kultur* on knowledge." He had been trying to believe in the possibility of a purely scientific *Kultur;* but at the same time, as a fact, he was struggling out of and beyond such intellectualism at the very moment he was trying to confess it. After the retirement of metaphysics he held that "a reactionary movement was necessary, in order to comprehend the historical justification, as well as the psychological, of such ideas, and to recognize that the greatest advancement of humanity must come thither, and how one is robbed of the best results of previous humanity without such reactionary movement." This sad knowledge-man now says, "The best in us is perhaps inherited from feelings of former times." "The sun has set," so speaks this man with his light of science, "but the heaven of our life glows and shines from the sun which we see no more." Nietzsche thus expresses a widespread sentiment of our own time.

The upshot of it all is that if man is no more than what the truth of science makes him out to be,—then, he can base his life not on truth but on error. "There are no longer free spirits," Nietzsche mocks in his *Genealogy of Morals,* "for they still believe in the truth."

Science requires for its knowledge universal validity, consequently impersonality. But every sentence of Nietzsche bears a personal color, a feature of his person. He praises "method" with his lips, but his impatient spirit hates to *reason* where he can *divine.* He hates "the new habit of comprehending, nonloving, nonhating, surveying," which is propagated by science. Once he said: *"Dem Lichte zu—deine letzte Bewegung: ein Jauchzen*

[131]

den Erkenntnis—dein letzter Laut." Now, in his third period, science is *eine Abard des asketischen Ideals,* a *Schleichweg zum nichts.* Knowledge is a flight from yourself, a sundering from will, a nihilistic movement. Science cannot stop until it reduces the rich, full, beautiful soul of man to physical reactions which can be experimentally determined and tested,—a greater reduction of man than Christianity makes! No wonder that Nietzsche hated both. Did he hate? Once in his second period he declared that the time would come when the *Memorabilia* of Socrates would replace the Bible. In his third period he calls Socrates the "rat-catcher of Athens." He passes the compliment around, for he says that Plato is a "decadent in style," "tiresome," "preëxistently Christian"; that Descartes is "superficial," "old"; Kant is an "insignificant psychologist," a "moral fanatic," "not in the least original"; his is a "backdoor philosophy," and Kant is "the most deformed conceptual cripple that ever existed." "Hegel, Schopenhauer, Spinoza! what poverty, what onesidedness!" Darwin, John Stuart Mill, Herbert Spencer— these are "mediocre Englishmen"! Mill is "an offensive transparency." Carlyle is an *"abgeschmackte Wirrkopf"* (unsavory muddlehead). Spencer's system is *"Krämer-Philosophie"* (shopkeeper philosophy).

We may close this chapter with the quotation of one of Nietzsche's most telling passages, and with a brief statement of the gist of the whole matter. Nietzsche says:

Compared with a genius, that is to say with a being who creates and conceives, in the highest sense of both words, the learned man, the scientific mediocrity, is something of an old maid; for, like the latter, he is unable to understand the two most valuable achievements of man. As a matter of fact, one recognizes both of them, the scientist and the old maid, as highly respectable. Let us examine more closely: What sort of person is the scientific man? First of all an essentially democratic specimen of mankind, with all the virtue of such a democratic specimen, that is to say of a man unable to command, incapable of exercising authority, incapable even of self-sufficiency. He is diligent, patient, orderly, moderate, always identical in his wants and in his capabilities; he has all the instincts of his race, and an instinctive desire for that which is necessary to men of his stamp . . . for instance, a modest independence and a green field, without which quiet, orderly work is impossible, honors and distinctions, the aureole of an honored and respected name which shall set the seal on his value and utility, the consciousness of which must always serve to repress the secret lack of confidence which ever lurks in the heart of every dependent man, of every gregarious animal. The scientist also has the malady and tares of an unaristocratic race: he is full of contemptible envy, and he has the eye of a lynx for detecting that which is base in the character of those to whose height he cannot attain.

Finally, two remarks should be made: First, according to Nietzsche Christianity is discredited. Why? Because all those passions and sentiments which enrich and ennoble and beautify life, "the affirmative sentiments, pride, joy, health, the love of the sexes, hatred and war, veneration, refined tastes and manners, a strong will, the cultivation of a powerful intellect, the Will to Power, thankfulness for the world and life, everything that brightens and adorns and divinizes for eternity, the whole force of illuminating virtue"—all these are condemned and persecuted by Christianity. Christianity, then, is done for because of its ascetic abridgment of life.

[133]

Secondly, what of our new faith, our faith in science? Is it a faith more favorable to the realization of Nietzsche's ideal than the old faith? Does science favor the development of the only life which is worth living, of the life which is strong, and powerful, and exuberant, and rich in creative power? Does science enable us to realize the only law of life, to live *wholly?* Precisely according to the determination of science as an aid or an obstacle to the realization of the great law of life must it be judged. And the verdict must be that science is an obstacle to its realization, and an obstacle scarcely less than Christianity itself.

Why? Look at the man of science. He is anything but a great man,—a reflector, but never a creator. He is a patient collector of details, a searcher after dusty archives and old manuscripts, a liver in library and laboratory; a specialist facing fossilization; without wide sympathies, varied tastes, or virile instincts, which are the features of the great man. His program favors the growth of a narrow spirit, of short-sightedness, fanaticism, ignorance, of everything except the leech's brain which he studies.

And science? It favors the intense development of commercialism and mercantilism, which regard the possession of wealth as the end of life. Science preaches the doctrine of equality, since it equalizes everything. It levels, it democratizes, it talks peace and platitude, well-being, happiness, charity, pacifism. If Christianity sets before its adherents an ideal which is nihilistic and anti-vital, modern science gives humanity an ideal which is, perhaps, even more ignoble, the ideal of wealth and material happiness as the justification and the end of life. It encourages ever-growing democratization, along with an ever-growing dearth of great men; the lack of a robust ideal; increasing industrial and commercial activity accompanied by increasing moral stagnation. Such is the net result.

Not *Fiat veritas, pereat vita!* therefore, but *Fiat vita, pereat veritas!* Coming out of his mountains where the granite kept company with the sky, thus again spoke Zarathustra!

CHAPTER NINE

NIETZSCHE AND ART

THE subject of this chapter is unusually difficult, for our Anglo-Saxon ideals are largely pragmatic and non-æsthetic. We can understand the intellectual point of view, and can work to increase knowledge and to establish truth. Then, too, we Anglo-Saxons are in the habit of emphasizing moral values. To us, the universe is a moral universe. With the rejection of morality, life would seem to lose all meaning, all worth. We may put aside religious creeds, cease to believe in heaven, lose all remembrance of the God of our fathers; but the moral law is still the ultimate; and it remains the ultimate, even although we change its content and regard it as the result of long development under purely natural conditions. We subject everything to a moral criterion, thrusting aside immoral art, and denying that it is art at all. The Anglo-Saxons are the only moral race, and therefore, the only hypocritical race.

Now, for the artistic standpoint, all this is changed. Moral and intellectual values cease to be sole values. Indeed, they become subordinate to others. The intellectual and moral life is no longer the only possibility. It is on a lower plane than the artistic life, where the law of beauty is recognized. Beauty is the supreme reason for existence. There is no necessity for a moral basis of the universe, which will do quite as well without it. Life is not a problem to be solved, or a task to be done. If the world is beautiful, why need we look further? Any amount of toil and hardship is justified if it produces only a little music, or painting, or poetry. One song compensates for all the tragedy of existence! Artists do not ask whether a book has a moral or an immoral tendency. They ask rather: Is it a work of art? Otherwise it deserves no consideration. Life for art's sake!

This point of view, of course, appears preposterous to the man to whom truth and goodness seem fundamental. But it was Nietzsche's point of view during the first period of his literary activity, that is, when he wrote *The Birth of Tragedy* and *Thoughts out of Season*. He even makes the artist the end and aim of the world. He regards the birth of tragedy as the most important moment in Greek history. He professes almost complete agreement with Schopenhauer's æsthetic theories. He gives to Wagner, the musician—music being the idiomatic expression of Schopenhauer's world-will—the supreme place in his dreams of the culture of the future. For Nietzsche, the ultimate questions are not moral, but artistic. As I say, it is not only art for art's sake, but life for art's sake; and life itself, as the old Greek held, is a work of art.

As I have pointed out previously, Nietzsche's philosophy had but one question, with three successive answers. The question was: If life is worth living, what is it that makes it so? Or, what is the supremely valuable? Art was his first answer; science was his second answer; art and morals being secondary, or rather, failing to interest at all. Artistic feeling gave way to critical keenness, and he questioned the validity of religion and morality and even logic.

His third answer—what was it?—*a transvaluation of all values*. He saw that, since he had once begun to question the standard of values, there was no way and no place to stop. He now sets aside the concept of truth itself; error has been of more value, he thinks. He keeps art, beauty, but holds that its biological function is just the opposite of what he held it to be in his first period. His third answer is of an ethical nature; yet it is supermorality, considered from the point of view of current or conventional morality. His position now is that *everything is of value that can further the development of the Superman*. The question now is, not whether a thing is beautiful or ugly, good or bad, true or false, but does it show and make a Will to Power; does it promote the end of the Superman? By Superman is meant power that is spirit, and spirit that is power. In a word, in this third period, a new standard of value is set up. And, as to our subject, whereas, in the first instance, art was valued as a consolation, a narcotic, an opiate, a hypnosis, a redemption, against the slings and arrows of outrageous fortune, now it is valued as a tonic to life, or, better, as a creator and creature of strength.

Have we now discovered, then, the way to know Nietzsche? First, he sees the insatiable and eternal unsatisfied will, which is the source of all misery, but redemption from the misery of this will through æsthetic idea and production, the artist being thus the ideal. Secondly, experiencing a great disillusion, he no longer finds the life-ideal in art, but in science. It is not the artistic man with his subjective constructions, but the scientific man with his objective thought, that is free and makes free. Espousing science, Nietzsche rejects his previous art ideal,

together with the will-philosophy, pessimism and nihilism
that were its presuppositions. In the only sunny years of
his life, he takes his stand on the soil of experience and
exact observation. Thirdly, he espouses the Will to Power,
the conflict of whose centers is productive of all values;
and the old Schopenhauer chloroforming of this conflict
becomes a crime against life. What produces or is a
product of strength is true or good or beautiful, if one
is to use such words, which, however, it is rather naïve
and virginal to do. Such are the contrasts! Is it, as a
German couplet has it:

> *Wer den Denker will verstehen*
> *Muss in Benkers Lande gehen?*

Nietzsche left the North and wandered long years in the
South, nightly pitching his moving tent a day's march
nearer, not home, but homelessness; a pilgrim and a
stranger of few and evil days, not attaining unto the
years of his father's in the days of the years of their pilgrimage, seeking a city which hath foundations, but
whose maker and builder was not God, but himself. The
wanderer lingered long in the South, and in the South
he brought his doctrine to its acme. I do not believe that
in the North he would have been in a position to let himself go so completely and riotously. But in the South life
pulsates differently in man and in nature. In the South
are other colors, other forms. In the South the opposites
and contrasts are more glaring. There, too, the transitions between life, with its beauty and bloom, and death,
with its terror and shadow, are harsher. There, in that
South, where the traces of the antique are everywhere in
evidence, was the memory of the *Imperium Romanum*,

the dear memory of the old Hellenic halcyon days, of the Greek temple, of Dionysos and Apollo, still living. There, in the South, equally, was there the memory of the Renaissance and its artist supermen full of life and power. And, all this, and such as this, echo and reëcho in Nietzsche's philosophy, with its contrasts and transitions as great as those from the apocalypse of Alpine snows and everlasting silence to the warmth of Neapolitan skies and the sunny joys of Italian life. I own to having all the more interest in Nietzsche because he ripened in such a clime, because his mind is not a series of syllogisms, his opinions not consistent, because his *leit-motif* was so manifold.

But we must turn quickly from such general considerations and come to closer quarters with our special subject. I do not know how we can better get forward than to ask ourselves, first, of *Nietzsche himself as an artist:* and, in more detail, secondly, again, of *Nietzsche's threefold evaluation of art.*

First, then Nietzsche, the artist: "We philosophers," writes Nietzsche to George Brandes, "are never more thankful than when we are confounded with artists." And critics, like Alois Riehl, are not entirely beside the mark when they assert that Nietzsche himself is an artist that one could confound with a philosopher. As we have seen, in his first youthful philosophy Nietzsche makes the existence of the world and of man an artistic achievement of the world-will. And his *Zarathustra,* a symbolistic philosophy-poem, signalizes the culmination of his creation. He tells us himself that but for a few outer contingencies, he would have ventured to have become a musician. And we know from his biographies that while still a child he was enthusiastic over the great masters of German music: Bach and Beethoven, Mozart and Haydn, Schubert and Mendelssohn, and later over Wagner especially, by whom he said "the world of music was for the first time circumnavigated." When about nine years old he began to compose little pieces of music; and improvising soon became one of his favorite amusements. He also worked seriously at the piano, and in time was able to play fairly well. While he gave up the thought of making music his career, a taste for music remained with him throughout his life. He seems to have been particularly attracted by all the obscure problems of musical æsthetics, which he considered with the double qualification of philosopher and artist.

In lieu of becoming a musician, he placed all his artistic qualifications, his musical abilities as well, at the service of language. Nietzsche was certainly a master over language: He used it as an instrument which obeyed his finest insights and every caprice of his temperament. He communicated his spirit to language—now the swift, now the serene, flow of his thought, and again the very color of his passion; and, as an artist makes his instrument express himself, so Nietzsche made language reveal his spirit. Reflection and ceaseless endeavor, not alone his inborn capacity, ripened in him this rare faculty of an artistic use of language.

Not quite language, but language as *poetry*, attracted. His sister has preserved a large number of his early verses, written between the ages of fourteen and twenty, testifying to delicate sensibility and a real gift for versification. Later on he wrote many poems, mostly of a philosophical character, with much dross indeed, but not a few grains of gold as well. Perhaps it was this practice of writing poetry that taught him to become such a fine prose writer. Nietzsche's sentences are evidently written and rewritten, chiseled with exquisite minuteness by a virtuoso of the pen, yet natural, sprightly, and graceful. His style would have none of your lumbering German sentences. It is passionate, lyrical; he never thinks with his intellect alone, but with his whole being. Does the reader not feel the presence of poet, painter, musician, especially musician, as well as philosopher, in *Zarathustra*?

In *Zarathustra* he says concerning "Reading and Writing":

Of all that is written, I love only what a person hath written with his blood. Write with blood and thou wilt find that blood is spirit.

In *Beyond Good and Evil* we find these words:

How may Germans know and require themselves to know, that art resides (*steckt*) in every good sentence—art which must be divined if the sentence is to be understood.

In *The Wanderer and His Shadow,* he writes:

None of the present day cultured nations has so bad a prose as the Germans. When the clever *blasé* Frenchmen say, "There is no German prose," we ought not to be angry, for this criticism is more polite than we deserve. If we look for reasons, we come at last to the strange phenomenon that the Germans know only *improvised* prose and have no conception of any other. The German simply cannot understand the Italian, who says that prose is as much harder than poetry as the representation of naked beauty is harder to the sculptor than that of draped beauty. . . . The notion of working at a page of prose as at a statue sounds to him like a tale from fairyland!

In *Beyond Good and Evil,* he cries:

What a torture are books written in German to a reader who has a *third* ear! How indignantly he stands beside the slowly turning swamp of sounds without tune and rhythms without dance, which Germans call a "book"! [And in the succeeding aphorism he continues:] The preacher was the only one in Germany who knew the weight of a syllable or a word, in what manner a sentence strikes, springs, rushes, flows and comes to a close. . . . The masterpiece of German prose is therefore with good reason the masterpiece of its greatest preacher: The Bible has hitherto been the best German book. Compared with Luther's Bible, almost everything else is mere "literature"—something which has not grown in Germany, and therefore has not taken and does not take root in German hearts, as the Bible has done.

As for Nietzsche himself, all artistic proclivities and talents have combined to produce uniqueness of style. Neitzsche is related to language as musician, poet, and painter at once. Musical charm of speech, literary painting—one can learn these from him. He knows the secret of painting with words and of bringing forms and colors before the fantasy of the reader. Let the reader consider the following passage from *Human, all-too-Human,* in which Nietzsche paints an Ober-Engadine landscape:

Et in Arcadia Ego—I looked down, over waves of hills, to a milky-green lake, through firs and pines austere with age; rocky crags of all shapes about me, the soil gray with flowers and grasses. A herd of cattle moved, stretched, and expanded itself before me; single cows and groups in the distance, in the clearest evening light, hard by the forest pines; others nearer and darker; all in calm and eventide contentment. My watch pointed to half-past six. The bull of the herd had stepped into the white foaming brook, and went forward slowly, now striving against, now giving way to its tempestuous course; thus, no doubt, he took his sort of fierce pleasure. Two dark brown beings, of Bergamasque origin, tended the herd, the girl dressed almost like a boy. On the left, overhanging cliffs and fields of snow above broad belts of woodland; to the right, two enormous ice-covered peaks high above me, shimmering in the veil of the sunny haze—all large, silent, and bright. The beauty of the whole was awe-inspiring and induced to a mute worship of the moment and its revelation. Unconsciously, as if nothing could be more natural, you peopled this pure, clear world of light (which had no trace of yearning, of expectancy, of looking forward or backward) with Greek heroes. You felt it all as Poussin and his school felt—at once heroic and idyllic.—So individual men too have lived, constantly feeling themselves in the world and the world in themselves, and among them one of the greatest men, the inventor of a heroic idyllic form of philosophy—Epicurus.

On the other hand, Nietzsche sketches a picture of a Böcklin kind in *Zarathustra:* "To be sure, I am a forest and a night of dark trees; but he who is not afraid of my darkness will find banks full of roses under my cypresses.

"And even the little God may he find who is dearest to maidens: Beside the well lieth he quietly, with closed eyes."

Here is an impressionistic sketch: "At an early hour, when the pail clinks down the well, and the horses neigh lustily through the green grasses. . . ." It is the mood of a morning ride you feel!

The poem *Autumn* is lyric, it is living music:

[144]

AND ART

Autumn

'Tis Autumn:—Autumn yet shall break my heart!
Fly away! Fly away!—
The sun creeps 'gainst the hill
And climbs and climbs
And rests at every step.
How faded grows the world!
In weary, slackened strings the wind
Playeth his time.
Fair Hope fled far—
He waileth after.

'Tis Autumn:—Autumn yet shall break my heart!
Fly away! Fly away!
O fruit o' the tree,
Thou tremblest, fallest?
What secret whispered unto thee
The night,
That icy shudders deck thy cheek,
Thy cheek of purple hue?
Silent art thou, nor dost reply—
Who speaketh still?—

'Tis Autumn:—Autumn yet shall break my heart!
Fly away! Fly away!—
"I am not fair,"—
So speaks the lone star-flower,—
"Yet men I love
And comfort men—
Many flowers shall they behold,
And stoop to me,
And break me, ah!—
So that within their eyes shall gleam
Remembrance swift,
Remembrance of far fairer things than I:—
I see it—see it—and I perish so."

'Tis Autumn:—Autumn yet shall break my heart!
Fly away! Fly away!

Or take this verse from the poem *The Sun Sinks*. It is
a Dionysian dithyramb of pure musical beauty:

The Sun Sinks

Rings nur Welle und Spiel.
Was je schwer war,
Sank in blaue Vergessenheit,—
Mussig steht nun mein Kahn.
Sturm und Fahrt—wie verlernt das!
Wunsch und Hoffen entrank,
Glatt liegt Seele und Meer.

The animation of nature-forms, once the source of
myths, is even to-day still the capability which evinces the
poet as such. Here is an instance of this from Nietzsche,
Between Birds of Prey:

Between Birds of Prey

Who would here descend,
How soon
Is he swallowed up by the depths!
But thou, Zarathustra,
Still lovest the abysses,
Loves them as does the fir tree!
The fir flings its roots
Where the rock itself gazes
Shuddering at the depths,—
The fir pauses before the abysses
Where all around
Would fain descend:
Amid the impatience
Of wild, rolling, leaping torrents

[146]

It waits so patient, stern and silent,
Lonely. . . .

Lonely!
Who would venture
Here to be guest—
To be my guest?
O bird of prey, perchance
Joyous at others misfortune,
Wilt cling persistent
To the hair of the steadfast watcher,
With frenzied laughter,
A vulture's laughter. . . .

Wherefore so steadfast?
—Mocks he so cruel:
He must have wings who loves the abyss,
He must not stay on the cliff,
As thou hangest there!—
O Zarathustra,
Cruellest Nimrod!
Of late still a hunter of God,
A spider's web to catch virtue,
An arrow of evil!
Now
Hunted by thyself,
Thine own prey
Caught in the grip of thine own soul.

Now
Lonely to me and thee,
Twofold in thine own knowledge,
Mid a hundred mirrors.
False to thyself,
Mid a hundred memories
Uncertain,

Weary at every wound
Shivering at every frost,
Throttled in thine own noose,
Self-knower!
Self-hangman!
Why didst bind thyself
With the noose of thy wisdom?
Why luredst thyself
Into the old serpent's paradise?
Who stolest into
Thyself, thyself?

A sick man now,
Sick of serpent's poison,
A captive now
Who hast drawn the hardest lot:
In thine own shaft
Bowed as thou workest,
In thine own cavern
Digging at thyself,
Helpless quite,
Stiff,
A cold corse
Overwhelmed with a hundred burdens,
Overburdened by thyself,
A knower!
A self-knower!
The wise Zarathustra! . . .

Thou soughtest the heaviest burden,
So foundest thou thyself,
And canst not shake thyself off. . . .

Watching,
Chewing,
One that stands upright no more!
Thou wilt grow deformed even in thy grave,

Deformed spirit!
And of late still so proud
On all the stilts of thy pride!
Of late still the godless hermit,
The hermit with one comrade—the devil,
The scarlet prince of every devilment! . . .

Now—
Between two nothings
Huddled up,
A question-mark,
A weary riddle,
A riddle for vultures . . .
They will "solve" thee,
They hunger for thy "solution,"
They flutter already about their "riddle,"
About thee, the doomed one!
O Zarathustra,
Self-knower!
Self-hangman!

To be sure, Nietzsche's peculiarly poetic work is *Zarathustra,* a happy imitation of Oriental poetry, the natural forms of the simple-sublime Wisdom Literature, approximating, not surpassing, the poesy and grandeur of the old Hebrew Psalms and Proverbs. We have now done with Nietzsche as artist,—Nietzsche with his aphorism, and lyricism, and symbolism, and mysticism. The other thing which we must consider is his philosophy of art.

Nietzsche's theory of art reposes at first upon Schopenhauer's, and Schopenhauer's on his will-metaphysics, and his will-metaphysics harks back to the ideology of Plato, and Plato's ideology is a fusion of the changeless being of Parmenides and the eternal flux of Heraclitus.

Nietzsche's starting point, then, is Schopenhauer's metaphysics. The essence of the world is will, says Schopenhauer, not simply conscious will, illumined by intellect, but everything will-like, yearning, desire, striving, the impulses and instincts of animals, growth of plants, force of electricity and gravity, and the like in inorganic nature. Not will is power but power is will.

This will is the Kantian thing-in-itself, with a difference. This thing-in-itself is extratemporal, extraspatial, extracausal. All this is not true of will as we know it. The will therefore as thing-in-itself is outside of space, time, and plurality. It is the all-one, undivided, original being.

All nature is will objectivized. But nature shows a gradation of types, each type specializing into a multitude of individuals. These types are the stages of the will's objectivization; types being what Plato called the unbecome ideas of things; what the Middle Ages called unbecome species; what Darwin meant when he said, not *unbecome,* but *origin* of species.

Now, the crucial question is: What does this architypal One, this All-Will underlying the phenomenal world—what does this All-Will *will?* Does this All-Will will a higher development of the world to distant goals, to far-off divine events? Does this All-Will will the perfection and spiritualization of culture? Does this All-Will will the moralization and ennoblement of humanity as the final end?

Nothing of the sort can the world-will will, since all goals, all culture, all ennoblement of humanity, have meaning and import only in the kingdom of the intellect, *i.e.,* only in the phenomenal world, but the will as thing-in-itself is will residing beyond phenomenon and intellect, reasonless will, therefore, will of necessity lacking conscious goals. What, then, does this will will, if it wills no goal? There is only one other thing it can do. *This will wills just to will, to live, to effectuate itself, to affirm itself. The will as kernel of phenomenon is will to live, that is, will to its own self.* But this will is necessarily a *suffering* will. Willing in general is unpleasant, for, as willing, it arises from want, need, discomfort. But since, now, the will knows no last goal of striving and must will to strive to all eternity, there is also no measure and goal of suffering. The will is the kernel of nature, of the world. Hence nature and the world are only vast abodes of pain,—less pain in the inorganic, more in the organic, most in man, and most of all in the genius, man's crown of glory. Such is the pessimistic basic view of Schopenhauer: to will without cause, to suffer generation after generation until our planet breaks up into fragments.

Now, such a world does not justify its existence; the amount of suffering is far greater than the amount of happiness. It is on this account that man should aim at the abolition of his will. This can be effected by art and by asceticism, by art temporarily and intermittently, by asceticism permanently.

But what can art do toward abolishing the will, even at times? Briefly stated, Schopenhauer maintains that the contemplation which is free from causality and will is the essence of the æsthetic life. In art, the intellect succeeds in freeing itself from the supremacy of the will, in laying aside the questions of the *why* and the *wherefore,* the *where* and the *when;* in sinking itself in the pure *what* of things. With most men, the intellect always remains a prisoner in the service of the will to live; but, in the artist, the intellect strips off all that is individual, and, in disinterested vision of the ideas, the Platonic Ideas, becomes pure timeless subject, freed from the will. Art removes individuality from the subject as well as from the object; its comforting and cheering influence depends on the fact that it elevates those enjoying it to the standpoint, raised above all pain or desire, of a fixed, calm, completely objective contemplation of the unchangeable essence, of the eternal Platonic types of things. Poetry, which presents most perfectly in tragedy the Idea of humanity, stands higher than the plastic arts. But the highest rank belongs to music of one of the stages; music, which is not a copy of the will's objectivization, but which is a copy of the will and so of the world essence itself; music, which utters the striving, yearning, craving, and the world-feeling conditioned thereby; music, the pure revelation of the metaphysical essence of the world in tones.

In sum, then, the value of art for Schopenhauer lies mainly in its power to deliver us from the slavery of the will. In the quiet contemplation of beauty revealed in art, we are delivered from the misery of life. Art provides us with a sphere in which we can escape from all our misery, and can attain to a state of temporary peace and painlessness. So Schopenhauer believed. So, with modifications, Wagner. And so, Nietzsche in his first stage. Wagner would heal the primal, metaphysical wound of humanity by the balm of his music; and Nietzsche applauded.

Then Nietzsche quite abruptly exchanged the pessimistic voluntarism of Schopenhauer for the optimistic and shallow rationalism of Socrates and Voltaire. But there can be only a metaphysic music, not a science music. Art has nothing to do with science—truth concerning the essence of the world. To give up metaphysics is to give up music. The new Nietzsche of positivism saw this. So he now teaches that the act by means of which, as one has hitherto believed, the artist sees the thing-in-itself to the bottom,—the act of inspiration,—is stripped of its prophecy by sober psychological research.

Is it, now, the tragic fatality of a sick soul, is it the demonic play of a spirit of negation, when precisely the very preacher of this grandiose art prophecy goes astray in his own preaching, when he finally thrusts it from him with shrill laughter? The poet-philosopher Nietzsche begins *to think* concerning his preaching. But art makes the thinker's heart heavy. Art constantly speaks a language which thought cannot express. Art strikes chords in the human heart, and there are at once intimations of a *Beyond* of all thought. The thinker Nietzsche now bade good-by to every *Beyond* of his thought. Nothing unthinkable was to be left for the feelings. So the thinker felt a stab in every art—a doubt whether he should cleave to the incomprehensible, or sell himself to the devil of the comprehensible!

Nietzsche now went forward into his third period, but backward to Schopenhauer again, with a difference, as we have seen. Schopenhauer's metaphysics was idealistic and monistic; Nietzsche's was realistic and pluralistic. Schopenhauer's world was One Will; Nietzsche's was multitudinous will—punctuations in everlasting, gladiatorial, kingly conflict—the source of values. Schopenhauer said Nay to life on account of its pain; Nietzsche said Yes to life with its pain, his own pain; and he said it with

Dionysiac, Bacchanalian ecstasy. Schopenhauer said the ideal man was will-weakness; Nietzsche said that the ideal man was will-strength.

Accordingly concerning art he now declared that Wagner's music sprang from weakness; that the art of the future was not to express and create the weakness of world-and-life-deniers, like ascetics and pessimists, but to utter and summon the strength of world-and-life-affirmers in their triumphal procession from *Vaterland* to *Kinderland!*

CHAPTER TEN

NIETZSCHE AND MORALITY

IN previous chapters I have indicated the seven characteristic, cardinal tendencies of Friedrich Nietzsche: Antimoral, antisocialistic, antidemocratic, antifeminist, antiintellectualistic, antipessimistic, and antichristian.

We are now concerned with Nietzsche's immoralism. Most people know little about Nietzsche except his watchword: *"Jenseits von Gut und Böse."* This is the affirmation that the usual distinction between good and evil is fallacious; that there must be the negation, or, rather, the transvaluation, of current moral values, that we must stigmatize our morals as *Widernatur,* that such morals must be replaced by the natural morality of the Superman —the Superman who drives through to the utmost his natural Will to Power, utterly regardless of our cheap pseudomoral evaluations. What your plebeian mob calls moral, and venerates as "sacred," is a fetish, which the strong and the enlightened despise. Nietzsche did not hold to the traditional distinction between good and evil. And, of course, we have to bear in mind that it is with reference to this distinction that we are entitled to designate his tendency as antimoralistic. For he replaces his negative destruction with a new positive table of values.

Again, we have wondered whether Nietzsche held to a basic principle from which these seven tendencies could be deduced, and thus explained. I believe that he did. And I still believe that it is in this basic principle that the peculiar kernel and the peculiar understanding of Nietzsche is to be found. Briefly put, as we have seen, Nietzscheanism is Schopenhauerism plus Darwinism. That is the *gist* of it, although, to be sure, it is too briefly put to be the full truth. Schopenhauer and Darwin each colored the other, and both were fused in the alembic of Nietzsche's own fiery and original personality.

I do not mean to deny that Nietzsche was deeply rooted in the past. He was. He knew the Greek sophists: Kallikles with his doctrine of the right of the stronger; his doctrine that moral and juristic restrictions are not from nature, but by precepts; his doctrine that laws are made only by the weak, the wretched, the many, as protection against the strong; his doctrine that all juristic and moral laws are unnatural fetters which the strong man snaps, without scruple and with a clear conscience, that he may fulfill the will of nature.

Nietzsche knew, moreover, the cynics; his own tendency, indeed, has been christened neocynicism. He knew the skeptics: *e.g.*, Anaxarchus, who fortified Alexander the Great, in the last grim movement of his folly, to be a Superman, and to exercise the right to rise above all restrictions.

Nietzsche knew the medieval Assassins and made their motto his own: "Nothing is true; everything is allowed."

Nietzsche knew the great individuals of the Renaissance and sought there the models of his Superman: *Machiavelli, Agrippa von Nettesheim, Montaigne.* He knew Thomas Hobbes (his English forerunner), with his "war of all against all." He knew not simply Mandeville in

England and the Encyclopedists in France, but especially Rousseau, preacher of a return to nature from the aberration and decadence of a higher culture. He knew Goethe and the genius-morality of the genius era. He knew Fichte with his *"Ich Chere,"* and Schlegel's malodorous novel, *Lucinde.* He knew young Germany, with Gutzkow's novel, *Wally,* and Mundt's novel, *Madonna.* And must he not have known Max Stirner, who used Hegel's dialectics to help him ridicule Feuerbach's philosophy of humanity, to help him substitute the individual ego for the abstraction humanity. . . . Max Stirner, whose book, *The Ego and his Own* became the program of the so-called *Edelanarchisten,* with whose leader, Kropotkin, Nietzsche's name has often been coupled?

Nietzsche ties up with this rich and interesting list of forerunners and is thus the representative of a tendency which breaks out from time to time throughout the history of culture, a tendency which always comes to the surface as an extreme reaction against a previous one-sided emphasis on the authority of human society over the individual and against the cultural exactions from the individual. In a word, all the world's long story of Nietzsches from the first rebel to the last is simply a reaction of *nature against culture (Kultur).*

We have seen that Nietzsche is Schopenhauer plus Darwin. But he is also the Nietzsche who has his kinship with this long line of spiritual ancestors—and yet who, in spite of this kinship, is a thoroughly original nature. There is a factor of underivability in him, as there is in every great personality.

Now, from Schopenhauer with his voluntarism, and Darwin with his intellectualism, in other words, from

voluntaristic Darwinism or from Will to Power (Schopenhauer's Will and Darwin's Power), can Nietzsche's immoralism be derived? When I say Darwin, I think of
Heraclitus, who believed that all development springs
from war and struggle. Darwin added but little in teaching that the struggle for existence is the condition of all
higher unfolding organisms; that the struggle strengthens
and the stronger triumph; that the weaker are driven to the
wall and deserve to go down. Nature wills the victory of
the strong and the defeat of the weak. This is the struggle
which Darwin adds to the blind centers of the will of
Schopenhauer.

Nietzsche is Darwin and Schopenhauer, but these modified; and I am willing to accept, though *cum grano salis,*
Peter Gast's view of the matter. Peter Gast, his assistant,
friend and disciple, writes:

> Nietzsche saw in nature, not the "will to life" (Schopen-
> hauer), but a will to the exaltation of life; not the "struggle
> for existence" (Darwin), but the struggle for a nobler,
> stronger existence; not the "instinct of self-preservation"
> (Spinoza), but the instinct of self-augmentation; not "love
> and strife" (Empedocles), but the contest for victory and
> supremacy.

With reservations hereinafter to appear, I accept this
formula of Peter Gast's, and revert to my point. Can
Nietzsche's immoralism be deduced from his basic principle? If the kernel and root of his doctrine be what I
have set forth, do all of those seven tendencies, against
so many traditional authorities (the antimoralistic just
now) flow with a sort of mathematical necessity from that
center? It seems to me that they do—all seven of them.
But we are now concerned with his immoralism.

[158]

Nietzsche's anti-intellectualism landed him in the position: "Nothing is true,"—the first half of those Assassin's watchword. His antimoralism landed him in the second half: "Everything is allowed." Nietzsche cited and praised this himself. This doctrine, of which the public has so much to say, constitutes only a part, but an important part, of his whole view of the world and of life. Nietzsche himself considered his ethics as a sort of subdivision of his physiology, or rather, biology. But, as a matter of fact, his antimoralistic tendency naturally and necessarily derives from his universal principle,—the Schopenhauer doctrine of the will under the influence of Darwinism. In the case of Schopenhauer himself, his ethical views necessarily counterbalanced his pessimistic metaphysics of the will. The single will-centers fight in a wild *"Gier,"* inflict all sorts of pain and woe upon each other until, according to Schopenhauer, the recognition of essential identity with the suffering brother ensues—and leads to the feeling of pity (*Mitleit*), of sympathy, with him, to helping him, so that out of this pity flow all the other virtues: love of neighbor (*Billigkeit*), righteousness! And this pity intensifies itself under certain conditions even to self-abnegation, even to self-effacement, yes, even to asceticism.

Now, from Nietzsche's point of view, which affirms the *will to live* and the *struggle for existence,* with important modifications, it is entirely consistent that Nietzsche, in opposition to Schopenhauer, should doubt, depreciate, and even deny the worth of those virtues: pity with the resultant neighbor-love, etc. We are not now concerned, of course, with the objective correctness of Nietzsche's judgment with reference to the evil of pity, but solely with the question whether his negation of pity consistently springs from his presupposition, from his basic principle of the Will to Power.

There are two lines of thought by means of which Nietzsche was led to his striking goal.

The first is a law of life that he looked upon as firm as a rock; namely, that the strong triumph and ought to triumph; the weak go down and ought to go down. "Death to the weak!" is a proverb with Nietzsche. It is an offense, therefore, a violation of the law of nature, to support and maintain what nature herself has destined to go down. Pity for the weak and miserable hinders, indeed, only their defeat as willed by nature. In alliance with the Darwinian doctrine of selection, mindful also, perhaps, of certain hard but useful institutions and customs of antiquity, Nietzsche demanded absolute pitilessness toward the weak; the way to their natural downgoing should be prepared for them; they should not be artificially preserved in life, to the torture of the weak and the hindrance of others. We should not oppose the natural selection of the stronger. What nature has destined to sink beneath the waves of being, man ought not to keep swimming upon the surface of the stream. What nature puts asunder, man should not unite: the strong, the capable of life,—and the weak, the incapable of life; the sound and the sick. The sick should at least have the courage to steal away from life. This is the new doctrine of hardness, the admonition against any coddling through pity. Nietzsche was never weary of his exhortation: "Be hard!" You make yourself needlessly weak and you weaken your life force, if you dedicate sympathy, pity, and love to those who are incapable of life. It is a difficult doctrine— this doctrine of hardness and hardening of the heart against the weak and miserable. But it logically and necessarily follows from the basic principle of Nietzsche. And it is psychologically understandable that it finds an echo on all sides to-day. There are many among us to-day who think that our lives are too soft—especially that our present institutions involve an overmeasure of humanitarianism. And the modern demand that we live a strenuous and not a sensuous life would meet with Nietzsche's full support. He stands primarily for the formation of a healthy, virile, strong humanity by means of the extirpation of all the weak and powerless. He wants us to perpetuate nature's work of selection, as Plato wanted this in his state. And Nietzsche is of the opinion that inopportune pity for the weak hinders nature's tendency of natural selection. "Death to the weak!"—that is his explicit watchword.

The second way which led Nietzsche to his harsh antimoral attitude is the historical. Progress of the history of the world, the higher ascent of culture, is, as he thinks, actually an effect of war, an effect of cruel regardlessness, of ambition and selfishness. Every big step of progress, we owe to great conquerors. But these conquerors, in what they did, never had any regard for moral commandments, never hesitated to do what traditional morality called *böse*. Take, for example, the Saxony wars of Charles the Great. Such mighty will-natures of the history of the world stand above and beyond the vulgar evaluation, according to childish notions, of good and evil (*böse*). The customary moral evaluation cannot be imputed to such master-natures and such hero-natures. In such cases, precisely those qualities enhance life which conventional morality rejects.

Of course, the masses of the many and the many-too-many (*Viel-zu-Vielen*), who live under the control of such master-natures, call their way *"böse,"* that is, personally objectionable to them; and they—these masses—call the opposite qualities of gentleness and consideration "good," that is, personally acceptable, agreeable, to them. But originally "good" meant *vornchen,* superior, excellent; and the good, originally, were just the masters and the rulers. Originally *"schlecht,"* "bad," meant the small, the petty; and the bad were originally just *die kleine Leute,* "small fry." It was only in the course of time that these words became converted into their opposites. At bottom, masters and master-qualities are good under all circumstances. It was a distorted reversal of this word "good" when it received the *kleinbürgerlichen Sinn* (popular meaning), which subsequent times attached to it; when it came to mean "mild," "kind," "considerate." The master and the master-nature dare not be mild, kind, considerate. Hardness and the greatest possible energy, the real master-qualities: these only the *kleine Leute* call "bad," because they suffer under such mastership. But the proof of the pudding is in the eating of it; *Kultur* was possible only through the conqueror, through masters and master-qualities.

It was in this way, on the basis of this supposed historical treatment, aided by a questionable philology, that Nietzsche arrived at his offensive affirmations in which he literally stood the previous moral evaluation on its head. He now urges the *Umwertung aller Werte.* With demonic, uncanny inerrancy, Nietzsche drew the consequence from his presupposition—his basic principle: Nature wills the right of the stronger. The strong will, therefore, rightly suppresses the weaker in the struggle for existence. It is on the basis of this presupposition that Nietzsche makes the distinction between *Herrenmoral* and *Sklavenmoral*. *Sklavenmoral* (an expression, by the way, that Schopenhauer had already used) praises and promotes mildness, regard, weakness, indulgence, pity; but these, says Nietzsche, are purely unnatural sentiments. *Herrenmoral,* on the other hand, is the master-conduct, grounded in nature itself, nature-willed, which has always made the weaker serviceable to the masters, with regardless energy, even with wild cruelty. From the standpoint of *Herrenmoral,* everything is "good" which is strong and makes strong. *Herrenmoral,* therefore, calls "good" bravery, courage, energy, and calls "bad" weakness, cowardice, submissiveness, resignation. To be beautiful, brave, strong, daring, ferocious, unscrupulous, hard, cruel: There is your master-man. "Good" is synonymous with brave, hard, daring, intrepid. But to be obedient, obsequious, fearful, weak, timid, degenerate: There is your slave. The moral law—what is that? A pure creation of the slaves and the oppressed, designed to protect them against the aggressions of the masters, invented as an instrument of combat, an instrument for subduing the ruling races, physically invincible. The slaves employ an ideological weapon, since they possess none other. Our moral law is the reflection of the character of the slaves and represents their conception of life as opposed to that of the masters. The marks of the slave, cowardice, timidity, obsequiousness, are elevated in the moral law to the rank of virtues and become, indeed, love of one's enemies, obedience to God, meekness of heart.

Nietzsche's own illustration tells the tale. The eagle

calls lamb-eating "good"; but the lamb calls it "evil." What need has the eagle for a law governing lamb-eating? But the lamb would like a prohibitive law, and would make it, if any were makable. That distinguishes Nietzsche's position from customary and traditional opinion. For master-men, the exploitation of the weak is self-evidently desirable. The origin of a bad conscience and the guilt-feeling Nietzsche assigns to the degenerating influence of the slave-morality. The acme of this depravation, thinks Nietzsche, is Christianity with its senseless, exaggerated conception of sin. The so-called bad conscience is merely ingrown fear and gratuitous, pathological self-torture! Sound men do what they must do, conformably with their nature, and with a good conscience. We culture-men have come to be like tamed domestic animals, and have lost our original instincts—have become tame and hopelessly mediocre, slaves of a misunderstood altruism, no longer our own masters,—herd-men, not master-men.

At this point my subject branches out into many collateral items, some of which I should like to pick up. For one thing, the reader will see to what Nietzsche's explanation of the moral law is opposed. The moral law is not exterior to man, nor superior to man. The world of morals does not dominate the world of nature, but *vice versa.*

Again, the moral law has no supernatural sanction, not being of divine origin. There is no such solid foundation for morality as the existence of God was supposed to be. No, it is certain that the moral law first originated with man—not even with nature. For the rest of nature is profoundly immoral. Both the supernatural and the natural origin of the moral law have been overthrown.

Thirdly, the moral law did not originate in either the Pure Reason or the Practical Reason of Kant, as the Utilitarian and Evolutionist schools have shown.

But is there not implanted in each one of us a moral law, identical in its ultimate aim for all time and all places, and does not this moral law speak to us through the voice of conscience? Does not our conscience command and we obey? If we disobey, does not our conscience torture us with reproaches?

Nietzsche's critique of conscience is scattered throughout his books; but, for all that, it is whole, complete, and rigorous. He questions the validity of conscience. What is conscience but the accumulation of our instincts—a derivative from heredity or education or habit? Conscience? Is not the conscience of one man, with certain ancestral influences behind him, different from that of another, with different ancestral influences? Will not the conscience of each, *i.e.,* his manner of thinking and reasoning, and of judging persons and things, be shaped accordingly? Conscience? Will the hooligan brought up in an atmosphere of filth and vice have the same conscience as a man educated and environed in cleanliness and nobleness?

But Nietzsche's originality inheres in this question: Why do you consider such and such an act to be right or wrong? Is the distinction between right and wrong valid? My conscience tells me it is right or wrong, you say. But why is your conscience called in as arbitrator? What claim has it to infallibility? Your conscience is a part of yourself; you, the whole, are fallible; then, can it, the part, be infallible? Conscience has been formed by all sorts of accumulations. How can a part of yourself be infallible? How can that part of a whole which is immoral be moral? By what standard do you judge the judgments of your conscience? By your mental habits? But your mental habits are simply the result of your heredity and education. And why do you obey your conscience? Answer me that, my friend! Is your obedience real or feigned? Do you listen to the voice of conscience as a hypocrite, who needs to cloak his vices with the mantle of virtue? Do you listen as a coward, afraid to probe your conscience to the bottom? Do you listen and obey as a soldier listens and obeys his officer, automatically, without reflecting? For there are many ways of listening to the voice of conscience.

But there is another question, says Nietzsche: Every judgment you make, or which you say your conscience makes: Is it disinterested, or is it selfish, egotistical? He writes: "You embrace your neighbor and have soft words for him. But I say unto you: Your love of your neighbor is but your love of yourself falsified." Nietzsche denies not merely the reality of altruistic sentiments, but the value of them. We are egotistical in our love; we are most thoroughly egotistical in our love for others, which is egoism, strengthened and fortified. We love others as a means of conquering them, as a means of seducing them. In a word, our love is but an expression of our Will to Power and of domination.

Now, if there is nothing but egoism, and if altruism is but a term devoid of reality, what becomes of the reality of the moral law, whose foundation is altruism? The Utilitarian school has maintained that the interest of all and the interest of each coincide in the long run. But, in the first place, this is reducing the categorical imperative to a mere calculation of profit and loss. In the second place, the interests of the individual are not always identical with the interests of society.

And Nietzsche urges another point, *viz.,* the extremely antinatural, antivital tendency of the moral law. Morality is the greatest enemy of life, and of all that is fundamental in life. What does morality ask us to do? Fight against our instincts, crush them, crush what lies at the very root of life, crush the conditions of life. The aim of life is more life! The strong man, the real man, loves life and is not afraid of it, loves all that life contains, its risks and adventures, its tears and sufferings, its disappointments and disillusions, as well as its joys and victories. And the great passions, all of them are but signs of an exuberant and healthy vitality, which seeks to break down the barriers imposed upon it by artificial means, such as the moral law, and which seeks the only life worth living, the *integral* life. For the great man, all the passions are equally legitimate, equally necessary to the affirmation of life, hate as much as love, revenge as much as sympathy, lust as much as chastity, anger as much as goodness.

The moral law? Is it from God? No, answers Nietzsche. From nature? No! From man? Yes! But not from the great man. From the little man, as a device of his weakness to maintain himself in life and to subjugate the great man in his greatness. But greatness is the only thing worth while. Therefore morality is a partial paralysis of life.

The moral law is thus another of the great obstacles to the realization of Nietzsche's ideal. The mere fact of causing man to subordinate his personality to an external power is in itself a hindrance to the integral life. If it be replied that man's conscience is not external to him, it must be answered that while it is not external to him in reality, it is an accumulation of prejudices, habits, and experiences, derived either from heredity or from surrounding environment. The conscience is commanding to man—in the name of what? Reason? But what sort of abstract entity is this reason? Is it any the less derivable than conscience? What is this command to obey the summons of conscience in the name of some higher power, of God, nature, or society, but the command of man to obey his prejudices, habits, experiences—in the name of what? In the name of his mental habits.

So declares Nietzsche. Is there an answer to him? I wonder. At all events I should like to try. But not just yet. For the present, Zarathustra:

"Then turned his ship's prow away from *Vaterland* and set sail through the midnight hurricane to distant seas, to *Kinderland,* where are the rainbows and bridges of the Superman!"

CHAPTER ELEVEN

NIETZSCHE AND SKEPTICISM

THE title of this chapter is not descriptive and accurate. Skepticism historically is tied up with two other words, dogmatism and criticism. Dogmatism is an uncritical faith in the presumptions of reason or *a priori* principles and declares the existence of things which cannot be experienced or proved. Skepticism takes the exactly opposite stand, and refuses concurrence in generally accepted conclusions. Criticism examines the material and the worth of knowledge, and inquires into the validity of its source. Briefly, then, dogmatism *affirms;* skepticism *denies;* criticism *asks.*

My subject is rather Nietzsche and Criticism, or Nietzsche and the Nature of Knowledge, Nietzsche as concerned with the questions: Is the object of knowledge real or ideal? Are the experienced object and the real object identical? Is the origin of knowledge empirical or rational?

Let us concern ourselves for a moment with defining epistemology (*Erkenntnistheorie*). This is a branch of philosophy, and philosophy's main business is "to arrive at a wise estimate of the world we live in, of ourselves and our ideas, and of the wise men's way of living." The philosopher is concerned with "life and its ideals"; concerned with "the relations between these two, reality and ideals." What is the relation between cause and worth, energy and value?

Consider the terms, metaphysics and criticism: metaphysics, the problem of being; and criticism, the problem of worthfulness. These are the two fundamental questions. What is true knowledge? we ask; and, how am I to know? What are moral goodness, beauty, wealth, good government?

Now epistemology comes under the head of *criticism*. Epistemology is concerned with investigating what knowledge is. What is the worth of your knowledge in terms of truth? We ask ourselves these questions: What is knowledge? How do we know? What is the knowledge-process? What must we do (or experience) in order to know? Most of all do we ask: Is what we have and call our knowledge really what we take it to be? Is our knowledge really knowledge? Is knowledge a human possibility?

It is with all this that epistemology has to do. Without it "we may know and not know that we know; or we may not know and not know that we do not know." Epistemology, if it could, would enable us "to know that we know when we know; and to know that we do not know when we do not know."

My present subject, then, being interpreted, is: *Nietzsche and the problem of Knowledge.*

I shall state in advance the point of view at which Nietzsche arrived. Knowledge is only a special instance of the Will to Power, like everything else. The result is a biologico-skeptical epistemology. Nietzsche treated knowledge from the point of view of Darwinian evolutionism. He applied vigorously the theory of natural selection to the domain of ideas. Our knowledge is not knowledge itself. Our knowledge is the expression of an adaptation to a certain environment. That which we know, or think we know, is a purely subjective creation. Or, rather, it is not even subjective, for the "subject" is itself a resultant. We have no knowledge of subject or object since we have no knowledge at all in the exact sense of the word. *That which we call knowledge is simply that which is useful to the species in its persisting.* Knowledge is a manifestation of the Will to Power of that species. Truth, then, is not characterized by immutability, by universality, by necessity. Our truths are not values in themselves, apart from those conditions under which the truths were created by the species. Our truths are just conditions of life for us. Necessary truths? Would we hold to the necessity of the existence of the human species? No? Then are the ideas, the knowledge, the truths created by the species simply for the species necessary? What we call truths even universal, necessary, "eternal" truths, are mere idiosyncrasies of a certain species, one among many.

And so those entities: "Thing-in-itself," "categorical imperative," "God," "truth,"—all of these are merely phantoms of our imagination. The most immediate reality, the only reality which is permitted us to know, is not an object on the outside of us or a subject on the inside of us, but *the world of our desires and passions*. All our deeds, wishes, and thoughts are, in the end, governed by our instincts, and these instincts all spring from one primordial instinct, the Will to Power. This Will to Power suffices to explain all the manifestations of life, knowledge among the rest. Every living thing—plant, animal, man —tends to increase its strength by securing a mastery over other beings, other forces. This continuous effort, this perpetual struggle, in which every being ceaselessly stakes its life in order to increase its power, is the fundamental law of existence. Hence if a man aspires to truth, it is by reason of a natural instinct which, to satisfy itself, impels him to act in a certain way. Truth, to which the scientist devotes his entire life, was first sought for by the Will to Power, which was tending to enlarge its sphere of domination. But Nietzsche would add that, through some singular aberration, man has come to worship as an ideal that which he himself created to answer one of his own needs.

Man should say: "I live to satisfy my instincts, and in virtue of that law I shall seek the good and the true so far as my Will to Power impels me." But instead of saying this man lays down as a principle: "The good and the true must be sought for themselves alone; good must be done because it is good; we must aspire to truth for the love of truth; man's life is of no value except in so far as he subordinates his egoistic interest to this ideal end; man must, therefore, in the name of his ideal, restrain his personal instincts, and look upon egoism as an evil."

Nevertheless, that man who so reasons, according to Nietzsche, is also impelled by instinct, it is true; for instinct is the final motive for all our acts, though this instinct be perverted.

This, then, is the gist of the epistemology at which Nietzsche finally arrived. But he passed through three periods, here as elsewhere. As in former chapters, so in this, I am compelled to outline the evolution of his thought. Otherwise, by merely taking into consideration any one period—for instance, the last only, as I have just now done—I should do harm to the totality of his thinking.

(a) Even in his early life Nietzsche's inclinations led him toward this most difficult branch of knowledge, this doctrine of the faculty of cognition. At Easter, 1867, when he was but twenty-three years old, he desired to have the doctor's degree conferred upon him, and handed in a dissertation entitled, *The Fundamental Schemas of the Imaginative Faculty*, which, however, was not accepted, owing to its "professing tenets not admissible at the University of Leipzig."

In *The Birth of Tragedy* and in a keen essay *Wahrheit und Lüge*, we find Nietzsche already impressed by the limitations of our cognitive power. Already, music is represented as a realization of Will. The books which follow evince a slow change. The word "will" is sometimes replaced by "nature." Nietzsche was gradually drifting into positivism. Truth and knowledge are, however, still very much subordinated to life, a subordination which, in some degree, he insisted upon throughout nearly the whole of his career.

At this time—this first period—truth was to Nietzsche a means by which mankind tried in some degree to abolish the *bellum omnium contra omnes*, by deciding on the truth of a few facts. Later on, this origin being forgotten, the existence of a sense of veracity is assumed (*Wahrheit —Wahrhaftkeit*).

The origin of logic is to be found in the fact that, whilst the truths were fighting amongst themselves, man was looking for the alliance and help of reason and reflection. Logic, therefore, is by nature superficial. "Every idea originates by putting into equation things that are not equal."

(b) Let us turn, next, to his second period, in which

Nietzsche, the Thinker, is at his zenith. Truth, knowledge, science are now held at a high value. His allegiance was given to these, in this his second period, his positivistic, his Apollonian period, his naturalistic period, from *Human, all-too-Human* to *Joyful Wisdom*. But, for all that, an unhappy suspicion of truth, a certain hesitancy, lingers over his new allegiance. Again and again there come birds of passage from the hot regions of the Dionysianism of his first period. And gradually the passionate desire of the fighter for culture returned. But the whirlwind had become a monsoon,—and we have the third period.

In this third period, there is no absolute truth to form a starting point. There is no pure cognition. Descartes' *"Cogito, ergo sum,"* is considered as unproved by the Nietzsche of the last period. It is only safe to say: *"Cogito, ergo est."* Consciousness is to Nietzsche only a guiding means, a weapon; but not an aim, not a measure. Untruths also have been useful to life. "Truth is that kind of error without which a certain species of living being cannot exist. The value for life is ultimately decisive."

This idea is not peculiar to Nietzsche. Zola expressed it in his *Lourdes*. Le Bon said it in his *L'Homme et Sociétés*. Pain is an intellectual phenomenon, a judgment viewing conceptions as harmful. Racial prejudices are useful conventions.

This will to knowledge, then, to truth—this is the Will to Power. And we see that at the end Nietzsche's fundamental view is that all cognition, knowledge, truth, is *a vital function, a servant of life*. And life is a function of the Will to Power. *Nietzsche's epistemology, then, is a biological evaluation of cognition on a metaphysical basis.*

And now we must look into the problem a little more in detail. What do we mean when we speak of possessing knowledge of things? We mean that our minds entertain certain beliefs which represent things as they are. We assume, first of all, that there are human minds; secondly, that there is an immense variety of things; thirdly, that there are in the human mind beliefs relating to some of these things; fourthly, that the beliefs in the mind may, and often do, represent those things just as they are. These are the assumptions. But, the question arises: What warrant is there for the accuracy of the assumptions and their implications?

Nietzsche attacks this problem, questioning the possibility of human knowledge. He says, in effect, that the human understanding is really criticizing its own fitness to serve as an instrument of knowledge. But can an instrument criticize properly its own fitness? What would be required in order to answer the question of human knowledge in a reliable and decisive manner? It would require some sort of higher creature endowed with absolute knowledge, both of things themselves and of our beliefs concerning them, in order to compare our beliefs with the things themselves, and so to determine their agreement or disagreement. Are there such higher creatures? We do not know them, and we ourselves certainly cannot carry out this required comparison between beliefs and things. We cannot step outside of our own minds and have a peep at things as they are in themselves, in order to compare our beliefs with things. We cannot be really sure, therefore, that we know reality or any part of it. We entertain beliefs, certainly; but whether our beliefs are true, who can say?

[175]

Our truths are man-made. Truth is not something which is already there, to be found or discovered; truth is something which has to be created. Beliefs are "useful," not "true." The distinction is not between "truths" and "errors," but between "useful" errors and errors that are not "useful." In his *Joyful Wisdom* Nietzsche declares: "Our trust in reason and its categories proves that experience has taught the usefulness of things to life. All knowledge is humanizing." And again, in *Beyond Good and Evil:* "A thing might be true even if it is injurious or dangerous in the highest degree; indeed, the essential constitution of reality might be such that a full knowledge of it might prove fatal, so that truth would have to be veiled, sugared, falsified, in order to make it endurable, that is to say, in order to make life possible." Thus he adds biology to skepticism.

Helpful, life-sustaining beliefs are of supreme importance, even if they be erroneous. What, forsooth, could be more important to man than the preservation of the species? These useful errors must, therefore, not be despised. Call them truths even, if that helps us to appreciate their value for life—provided that we bear in mind that our stand point is anthropocentric, and that we do not set up human idiosyncrasy as the final measure of reality.

But can we not transcend the merely human standpoint? No, says Nietzsche. What happens here is very like what happens in the familiar phenomena of perspective. We may "know" that the picture before our eyes is flat, is in one plane only, and yet, on looking at it, we cannot help "seeing" three dimensions. We cannot help it, we are made to see such things that way. So the philosopher, who has reflected on the humanism of human knowledge, cannot liberate himself from the human perspective. "We cannot see around our corner," says Nietzsche. "It is hopeless curiosity to want to know what other modes of intellect and perspective there might be; for example, whether any kind of being could perceive time backwards, or alternately forwards and backwards, whereby another direction of life and another conception of cause and effect would be given. Yet the world may contain infinite perspectives and interpretations."

Such is Nietzsche's theory of knowledge. It is not particularly cheerful. By way of criticism two things might be said:

(1) Grant that the validity of human knowledge cannot be *proved*. But not to *prove* is not yet the same thing as to *disprove*. Human knowledge is *possible,* therefore.

(2) Grant that knowledge is only the peculiar way in which the world appears in human perspective. Yet man, and therefore the human perspective, is real enough. Consequently human knowledge is true so far as it goes, even if it is not the whole truth.

But, criticism aside, we have to admit that Nietzsche accepted the more cheerless alternative; namely, that for man there is probably no real truth or knowledge. But he rightly held that the problem of our time is the true apportioning and regulating of knowledge and life. As I say, he combined voluntarism and empiricism, skepticism and biology. Nietzsche was a skeptic. Skeptics are like thunderstorms; they pass, but they clear the air.

CHAPTER TWELVE

NIETZSCHE AND RELIGION

BEFORE passing to the consideration of the present theme, it may be well to give a brief *résumé* of Nietzsche's attitude toward religion, especially toward Christianity. Since Voltaire and Feuerbach, religion, and especially Christianity, has had no opponent so sharp and inexorable as Nietzsche, although himself a profoundly religious man in his own way. Nietzsche's book, *Antichrist,* is the keenest invective against Christianity that can be imagined. Naturally, Nietzsche looks upon Christianity as the strongest bulwark against his own doctrine. For Christianity is the exact counterpart of all the tendencies which we have found in Nietzsche. For example, Christianity is pessimistic as regards the world of sense. Christianity is democratic: it has a certain kinship with socialism, and with feminism. But the most important thing is his opposition to the morals of Christianity. Christianity teaches pity, love, self-denial, to the point of asceticism, especially nurture and care of the sick, the weak, and the miserable. Christianity acknowledges no right of the stronger; but, rather, conversely, the right of the weaker to consideration and pity. It is on this account that Nietzsche, consistently enough from his point of view, discovers in Christianity the original root of all decadence. Does Christianity triumph? Then the mass of the weak, of slaves, triumph over the few strong ones, those who are called by nature to be lords of the masses. It is in this sense that Nietzsche calls Christianity a *Sklavenaufstand der Moral,* a slave-uprising of morality. He seeks to show historically that Christianity was at first accepted and spread by slaves. Now, this slave-religion and slave-morality lauds, naturally, only those virtues which are useful to slaves: pity, love, consideration. But it taboos inconsiderateness, selfishness, and cruelty. Indeed, Christianity invented these abusive words for the relative natural virtues of the uncorrupted man: courage, energy, ambition, Will to Power. These latter are the virtues of the ancients, of the noble Greeks and Romans. Without these virtues the *Imperium Romanum* could never have been founded. But these virtues were restamped as vices by the slaves and their new Christianity. This false, unnatural transvaluation of natural values was brought about by Christianity. And on this account that glorious *Imperium Romanum* sank into dust, and the antique culture vanished. Hence the task of the present and of the future is to restore the natural evaluation, through an *Umwertung aller Werte*—all values which have gained validity since the rise of Christianity.

We have seen that Nietzsche's basic principle was a positive turn of Schopenhauer's doctrine of the will, under the influence of original Darwinism. Now it is from this principle that Nietzsche's antireligious, or better, antichristian attitude takes its rise. Schopenhauer assumed no such unfriendly bearing toward religion, especially toward Christianity, as has been commonly supposed. I venture to say, on the contrary, that none of our modern philosophers has penetrated so deeply into the essence of Christianity as has Schopenhauer, and no one has so warmly defended the very kernel of this religion as he has. Let the reader compare what Kant, Fichte, Schelling, Hegel, Herbart, and even Schleiermacher, have said concerning Christianity with what is found in Schopenhauer, and he will be convinced of the truth of the foregoing statement.

In particular, there are three fundamental ideas of Christianity that are most deeply regarded by Schopenhauer. These three ideas are *evil* (Böse), *love,* and *contempt of the world.* (a) *Evil,* in the sense of both physical and moral evil, plays a cardinal rôle in Schopenhauer. Why should he not, then, approach the analogous, fundamental idea of Christianity with great insight? (b) *Love* crops up in Schopenhauer as *pity* (*Mitleid*), pity being with Schopenhauer the universal principle of morality. (c) *Contempt of the world,* and its consequence, *world-flight,* first found their philosophic explanation and justification through Schopenhauer. How little intelligence do the other philosophers show in what they have to say concerning monasticism, asceticism, and virginity, as compared with Schopenhauer, with his profound explanation of these phenomena! We could extract from Schopenhauer an entire apology for Christianity, much as it is true that from other points of view he drove with a vengeance against Christianity, and especially against Judaism, the foundation of Christianity.

But no such apologetic attitude toward Christianity is to be expected from Nietzsche. It was precisely that positive turn which he gave to Schopenhauer's doctrine of the will, under the influence of original Darwinism, that conditioned his negative bearing toward Christianity.

In view of what has been said already about the natural

virtues,—courage, energy, ambition, regardlessness,—naturally Nietzsche would be offended by the pessimism of Christianity. Especially did he find it impossible to share Christianity's fundamental idea concerning moral evil, or sin. Indeed, he was convinced that it was precisely this sin-idea which was the peculiar destroyer of the freshness of life and the joy of life. Priests seemed to Nietzsche as the falsifiers of life's values, as the falsifiers of conscience. Priests called the natural, the instinctive, the original, sin! But cowardice, dolelessness, energylessness, bloodlessness, —priests called these virtues! They substitute their pale virtues for blooming and blowing life. They scorned bodily life. They prefer bloodless shadows to bodily life. Nietzsche rejected with wild violence this whole pessimistic conception of man and of life, from top to bottom.

But equally as little can Nietzsche abide the second fundamental idea of Christianity, the idea of love. *"Liebe ist Mitleid, Leben, aber ist Mitleidlosigkeit"* (Love is pity, but life is pitilessness). Life is conflict, war; only conflict and war are life-promoting. But Christian love extirpates these natural tendencies which rightly demolish those incapable of life and preserve only those capable of life. This second fundamental idea of Christian love is even contranatural from Nietzsche's standpoint.

Especially is this true of the third idea of Christianity, contempt of the world, flight from the world. Such a procedure is ingratitude to nature, he thinks—to nature in the midst of which we stand, and whose children we are. Nature has destined us to be warriors, and to be creators. But Christianity would rob us of the joy of war, and of the lust for creation. Work on the world, and on ourselves—this is what we ought to do in order to give the meaningless earth a meaning. Christianity rejects this world as world, as the secular, and bids us yearn for an invented and imaginary hereafter, for the sake of which we forego duty to shape existence here to the best of our ability. Christianity makes us slaves of a fictitious God, rather than lords ourselves of this real world.

So Nietzsche fought Christianity, and all religions, with rare bitterness. And it would be impossible for one to accept his fundamental principle and not think as he did on this matter. Nietzsche is to be met only by correcting his fundamental principle, on the one hand; and, on the other, by pointing out that he partly misunderstands and misinterprets Christianity—especially that he is wrong in identifying the essence of Christianity with a single historical form of its manifestation. But this important criticism is not my concern just now. Having indicated his judgment touching these three ideas: Christian pessimism, pity, and asceticism, erroneously supposed to be the essence of this religion, I am now to isolate pity and pity-morality from this complex, and devote the rest of the chapter to its examination.

But the reader would like to hear Nietzsche speak for himself first of all. My quotations shall be as fairly representative as I can make them.

There is an autobiographical statement in his *Ecce Homo* which is unusually interesting:

My experience [he writes] gave me a right to feel suspicious in regard to all so-called "unselfish" instincts, in regard to the whole "neighborly love" which is ever ready and waiting with deeds and with advice. To me it seems that these instincts are a sign of weakness, they are an example of the inability to withstand a stimulus—it is only among decadents that this pity is called a virtue. What I reproach the pitiful with is, that they are too ready to forget shame, reverence, delicacy of feeling which knows how to keep at a distance; they do not remember that this gushing pity stinks of the mob, and that it is next of kin to bad manners—that pitiful hands may be thrust with results fatally destructive into a great destiny, into a lonely and wounded retirement, and into the privilege with which great guilt endows one. The overcoming of pity I reckon among the noble virtues. In the Temptation of Zarathustra, I have imagined a case in which a great cry of distress reaches his ears, in which pity swoops down upon him like a last sin, and would make him break faith with himself. To remain one's own master in such circumstances to keep the sublimity of one's mission pure in such cases,—pure from the many ignoble and more short-sighted impulses which come into play in so-called unselfish actions,—this is the rub, the last test perhaps which a Zarathustra has to undergo—the actual proof of his power.

In *Human, all-too-Human,* we have his first thought on the subject. He says: "La Rochefoucauld assuredly hits the nail on the head when he warns all sensible people against pity." He reminds us that both La Rochefoucauld and Plato held that "pity weakens the soul,"

Live in intercourse with the sick and the mentally depressed [he continues], and ask yourself whether that ready complaining and whimpering, that making a show of misfortune, does not, at bottom, aim at making the spectators miserable. . . . The weak and suffering see that they still possess one power, in spite of their weakness, the power of giving pain.

A little further on he makes this important analysis:

Pity aims just as little at the pleasure of others, as malice at the pain of others *per se.* For it (pity) contains at least two elements of personal pleasure, and in so far, self-gratification; in the first place as the pleasure of emotion, which is the kind of pity that exists in tragedy, and then, when it impels to action, as the pleasure of satisfaction in the exercise of power. If, besides this, a suffering person is very dear to us, we lift a sorrow from ourselves by the exercise of sympathetic actions. Except by a few philosophers, pity has always been placed very low in the scale of moral feelings, and rightly so.

Plato, Aristotle, Spinoza, Kant, were all against pity, had contempt for pity. Mandeville in *The Fable of the Bees* calls pity a frailty and finds vice beneficial, for "virtue can't make nations live."

There is an important passage in *The Genealogy of Morals,* in which Nietzsche tells of his first interest in the subject of pity, of which he wrote in *Human, all-too-Human:*

I had set my heart, at that time on something more important than the nature of theories . . . concerning the origin of morality. . . . The issue for me was the *value* of morality . . . the issue was, strangely enough, the value of the *"unegoistic"* instincts, the instincts of pity, self-denial, and self-sacrifice, which Schopenhauer had so persistently painted in golden colors, deified and etherealized, that eventually they appeared to him, as it were, high and dry, as "intrinsic values in themselves," on the strength of which Schopenhauer uttered both to life and to himself his own negation. But against *these very instincts* there voiced itself in my soul a more and more fundamental mistrust, a skepticism that dug ever deeper and deeper; and in this very instinct I saw the *great* danger of mankind, its most sublime temptation and seduction—seduction to what?—to nothingness?—in these very instincts I saw the beginning of the end, stability (stationariness?), the exhaustion that gazes backwards, the will turned *against* life, the last illness announcing itself with its own mincing melancholy. I realized that the morality of pity which spread wider and wider, whose grip infected even philosophers with its disease, was the most sinister symptom of our modern European civilization; I realized that it was the route along which that civilization slid on its way to—a new Buddhism?—a European Buddhism?—*Nihilism?* This exaggerated estimation in which modern philosophers have held pity is quite a new phenomenon; up to that time philosophers were absolutely unanimous as to the worthlessness of pity.

Again, there is the following thought from his *Joyful Wisdom:*

"The lust of property and love: what different associations each of these ideas evokes!—and yet it might be the same impulse twice named. Our love of our neighbor—is it not a striving after new *property?*"

But let us pass to some of Nietzsche's deadlier rapier thrusts. In *Zarathustra,* under the heading, "The Pitiful," we find these words:

Verily, I like them not, the merciful ones, whose bliss is in their pity: too destitute are they of bashfulness. . . .

Where in the world have there been greater follies than with the pitiful? And what in the world hath caused more suffering than the follies of the pitiful?

Woe unto all loving ones who have not an elevation that is above their pity!

Thus spake the devil unto me once on a time: "Even God hath his hell: it is his love for man." And lately did I hear him say these words: "God is dead: of his pity for man hath God died."

So be ye warned against pity: *from thence* there yet cometh unto men a heavy cloud! Verily, I understand weather-signs!

But attend also unto this word: All great love is above all its pity; for it seeketh—to create what is loved!

Myself do I offer unto my love, *and my neighbor as myself*—such is the language of all creators.

All creators, however, are hard.

In the *Will to Power,* Nietzsche speaks of pity as Christian moral quackery: "Pity and contempt succeed each other at short intervals, and at the sight of them I feel as indignant as if I were in the presence of the most despicable crime." Again he says: "Pity is a waste of feeling, a moral parasite which is injurious to the health."

Perhaps Nietzsche's whole criticism of pity is summed up in this passage from his *Antichrist:*

Christianity is called the religion of *pity.* Pity is opposed to the tonic passions which enhance the energy of the feeling of life: its action is depressing. A man loses power when he pities. By means of pity the drain on strength which suffering already introduces into the world is multiplied a thousandfold. Through pity, suffering itself becomes infectious; in certain circumstances it may lead to a total loss of life and vital energy. . . .

Supposing one measures pity according to the value of the reactions it usually stimulates, its danger to life appears in a much more telling light. On the whole, pity thwarts the law of development which is the law of selection. It preserves that which is ripe for death, it fights in favor of the disinherited and the condemned of life; thanks to the multitude of abortions of all kinds which it maintains in life, it lends itself a sombre and questionable aspect. People have dared to call pity a virtue, though in every noble culture it is considered a weakness. People went still further, they exalted it to *the* virtue, the root and origin of all virtues,—but, of course what must never be forgotten is the fact that this was done from the standpoint of a philosophy which was nihilistic, and on whose shield "The Denial of Life" was inscribed. Schopenhauer was right in this respect: by means of pity life is denied and *made more worthy of denial,*—pity is the *praxis* of nihilism. I repeat, this depressing and infectious instinct thwarts those instincts which aim at the preservation and enhancement of the value of life: by *multiplying* misery quite as much as by preserving all that is miserable, it is the principle agent in promoting decadence,—pity exhorts people to nothing, to nonentity! But they do not say "nonentity," they say "Beyond," or "God," or "True Life"; or "Nirvana," or "Salvation," or "Blessedness," instead. Schopenhauer was hostile to life: that is why he elevated pity to a virtue. . . . Nothing is more unhealthy in the midst of our unhealthy modernity than Christian pity!

But most important of all is the fact that Nietzsche's faith in morality began to wane when he doubted the worth of pity. The problem of the worth of pity widened, I mean, to the problem of the worth of morality at all.

And once more he shall speak for himself on this important matter. In *The Genealogy of Morals* he writes:

This problem of the value of pity and of the pity-morality seems at the first blush a mere isolated problem, a note of interrogation for itself; he, however, who once halts at this problem, and learns how to put questions, will experience what I experienced: a new and immense vista unfolds itself before him, a sense of potentiality seizes him like a vertigo, every species of doubt, mistrust, and fear springs up, the belief in morality, nay, in all morality, totters—finally a new demand voices itself. Let us speak out this *new demand*: we need a critique of moral values, *the value of these values* is for the first time to be called in question. . . . The value of these "values" was taken for granted as an indisputable fact, which was beyond all question. No one has, up to the present, exhibited the faintest doubt or hesitation in judging the "good man" to be of a higher value than the "evil man," of a higher value with regard specifically to human progress, utility, and prosperity generally, not forgetting the future. What? Suppose the converse were the truth! What? Suppose there lurked in the "good man" a symptom of retrogression, a poison, a narcotic, by means of which the present battened on the future! More comfortable and less risky perhaps than its opposite, but also pettier, meaner! So that morality would really be saddled with the guilt, if the maximum *potentiality of the power and splendor* of the human species were never to be attained? So that really morality would be the danger of dangers?

Such, it is fair to say, is Nietzsche's view. Sympathy adds to the number of those who are miserable. Those who are happy, who love life, who cherish life,—these are sure to be rendered unhappy, are sure to be turned against life, to declare life a misery and a burden, by sympathizing with those who are miserable and who hate life because they are miserable. For what is sympathy? It is the sharing of another's burden; only, this sharing of the burden does not relieve any of the weight on the shoulders of him who is miserable, while it places a burden which was hitherto absent on the shoulders of him who was up till then happy. Sympathy, then, adds to the stock of ugliness and suffering in the world. Schopenhauer was right when he saw in sympathy the best means of attaining to that negation of the desire to live which he prized as the highest wisdom. Sympathy reveals to us the depths of the world's suffering and inspires us with timidity in the face of suffering, with the consciousness of the nonvalue of life. Sympathy incites us to desire the cessation of all life, the cessation of all desire. Thus, sympathy is an antivital sentiment. And it was but natural that Nietzsche, the great apostle of life in all its plenitude, should regard sympathy as a crime.

Zarathustra is hard. He is egotistical. He seeks the integral development of his personality. He knows neither pity, nor sympathy, nor tender-heartedness, nor justice. He knows but one law; and that law is his own law, the law of his own force, the law which is at once its own sanction and its own delimitation. Zarathustra's greatest trial is the trial of his sympathy, that shall show whether he is capable of placing a new table of values before humanity. The reader should read Nietzsche's "The Ugliest Man." Zarathustra meets suddenly, in a vile place where nothing grows and only serpents are to be found, a repulsive and awful-looking object, the most hideous of men, him who represents all the accumulated load of humanity's sufferings and misfortunes, him who has slain God by his very hideousness; for even God could not look with impunity on so much hideousness and misery. And when he first sees this awful-looking object, Zarathustra has a moment's hesitation, he endures for a moment the distress of uncertainty and poignant anguish, and then he falls to the ground. But it is only for a moment. The combat is swift and deadly, but Zarathustra is capable of surmounting himself. He rises again after a minute, his heart steeled against all pity, and goes on his way. Zarathustra has vanquished pity; Zarathustra has withstood the spectacle of the Most Hideous Man, of him whose very hideousness has slain God; and Zarathustra has emerged stronger than ever from the ordeal. Pity and sympathy have been crushed; and the new table which

Zarathustra has come to place above humanity has been sanctified: *Werdet Hart* (Become hard).

But we must now attack the critical question: What is the *value* of Nietzsche's doctrine here?

I find that many of Nietzsche's opponents convict him of a contradiction, and dismiss him with that, rather summarily. On the one hand, Nietzsche indicts pity because it augments suffering; on the other hand, he teaches that it is in the school of suffering—of intense suffering—that has been created every great thing which humanity has produced. But the contradiction is more apparent than real. The suffering that comes from pity springs from weakness and makes weak. The other suffering, which Nietzsche lauds, is not something done to life, but something that life itself does in connection with its creation of values. The soul becomes strong, not weak, by such suffering, by facing catastrophes, by utilizing misfortunes.

Other critics urge that Nietzsche's total rejection of Christian morality is not warranted by an appeal to its fruits. But Nietzsche, I would say in reply, does not seek the annihilation either of the Christian religion or of morality in general. He merely seeks, and seeks passionately, to destroy the monopoly attaching to the Christian religion and to morality. According to Nietzsche, Christianism and the moral law are the creations of inferior races, of the slaves, the *bourgeoisie*. For the slave and the *bourgeoisie* were they created; they respond to an urgent need of these classes, and for these classes they are in many respects a boon. But, of course, Nietzsche says that the superior elements are above and beyond Christianity and the moral law. It may not be amiss to inquire whether many "slaves," to use his word, are not presuming to live according to the master-morality of the Superman—a morality for which they are not competent, and are consequently going to moral ruin through their presumption. Nietzsche, I am sure, would consign many a boasted master-moralist trying to be his disciple to-day to the slave-morality where alone he would accord him respect.

But I desire just here to point out that critics are mistaken in declaring that Nietzsche totally rejects so-called Christian morality. He rejects it only for the masters, not for the slaves.

Now, as against these critics, I find something valuable in Nietzsche's doctrine of hardness and antisympathy. Nietzsche's doctrine supplies a distinct want in the mental atmosphere of the time. In an age whose watchword in politics is democracy, and in ethics self-sacrifice, it is well to be reminded that aristocracy and self-assertion are not synonymous with evil. Even an ideal democracy would hardly be an unmixed blessing, while its actual form leaves still more to be desired. Self-sacrifice, if consistently adhered to, results in a personality that ought to be sacrificed, the sooner the better. If life is to be maintained at all, there must be some self-assertion; and much more is necessary if the life is to be worthy of maintenance. Humility and abnegation have had more than their due share of glory. The warlike virtues of the soldier are incomplete, but not therefore vices. Lack of strength in the individual is not to be compensated by any amount of general comfort. A vigorous personality is more to be desired than self-effacement. Pain, like poverty, is not so bad as the want of power to endure it. We cannot afford to ignore the bracing, stimulating side of Nietzsche's view of life, his exposure of softness, of flimsy and sugary sentimental-ism, of our slipshod temper, of the mental atmosphere of the slacker. He puts iron into our blood and keys our souls to those high thoughts that wander through eternity. And in this respect I side with Nietzsche against his misunderstanders and some of his critics.

But for all that, much that he says upon pity-morality indeed upon morality in general, gives me pause.

For one thing his conception of pity, of sympathy, is defective. By pity Nietzsche understands, above all, the passive, sentimental form of sympathy, which weakens both the sympathizer and the object of his pity. Now this is an inadequate idea. It is to say that sympathy is only physiological, psychological, whereas it is also ethical and spiritual. For another thing, Nietzsche misunderstands the gospel when he identifies pity-morality with the morality of Jesus. Indeed, Jesus never said anything about pity in the Schopenhauerian, Buddhistic sense that Nietzsche has in mind—unless one makes an exception (which I do not) of, "Blessed are the merciful, for they shall obtain mercy."

Nietzsche, in his last letter, written to George Brandes, signed himself "The Crucified." But when Jesus was climbing Calvary actually to be crucified, the women of Jerusalem followed him weeping. Jesus turned upon them and said: "Daughters of Jerusalem, weep not for me!" Lonely, defeated, humiliated, Jesus rejected the Nietzschean pity. Nietzsche is especially wide of the mark when he identifies pity and the Christian love. What is that love? I will quote an example:

I may have such absolute faith that I can move hills from their place, but if I have no love, I count for nothing; I may distribute all I possess in charity, I may give up my body to be burned, but if I have no love I make nothing of it.

Love is very patient, very kind. Love knows no jealousy; love makes no parade, gives itself no airs, is never rude, never selfish, never irritated, never resentful; love is never glad when others go wrong; love is gladdened by goodness, always slow to expose, always eager to believe the best, always hopeful.

That is the kernel of the Christian morality; it is not pity in Nietzsche's phrase. It is ethical, and more difficult than a life red in tooth and claw. For myself, I am not ashamed to say that I would not care to live in a world from which love, so understood, is absent.

But for another thing still, I raise the question whether the Nietzschean pitiless hardness would not result in waste which would be antibiological. For the sake of the argument, let us grant that our humanitarianism is keeping in existence human worthlessness that ought to be wasted, human life that ought to be extirpated by some form of euthanasia. Still there is difficulty here. How little must I be worth to society to be worth nothing at all? Besides, is no worth-while character matured by strength serving weakness? Besides, again, if Nietzschean hardness had been put into effect would not Nietzsche himself have been lost to the world—and many another genius? How many a baby that did not seem worth the care it cost has turned out to be a social asset? And so I might go on. We are here to save life, not to destroy it; that is the rule, whatever the exceptions may be. Back of everything else, I have an idea that power which can only be powerful through physical self-expression is not so great and fine as that other power which can also express itself by self-inhibition. For a man to keep pace with a little child is more powerful than for him violently to make a little child keep pace with him.

Nietzsche appeals, however, to Darwinian natural selection, and says it is violated as a weeder-out of human worthlessness by our humanitarianism. We must not interfere with the natural struggle for existence and its natural consequences. This I do not believe. Huxley, as honest a scientist as Nietzsche is a philosopher, reminded the crude exaggerators of the theory of evolution that the "cosmic struggle" is not the last word of nature; that *with* man, if not *before* man, begins the "ethical process" of which love is the inner force; that, in the correction and mastery of the natural,—the fang and claw struggle, the brute upthrust of existence,—by the ethical, the harmonizing, the sharing, and protective instincts, lies all hope for any development worthy of the name. It is only this *leavening grip of otherness* which effects the social transformation that can give love a home within the world's heart and soul. In helping on this higher process we are hastening the day when, through no shunning of hardship or shrinking from conflict, but through the carrying of the principle of struggle onward into the region of will and spirit, man may have left behind him the agony of the past, red in tooth and claw, and the birth-throes through which he mounts into a clearer air and a wider world beneath serener skies.

Finally, Nietzsche's hard-and-fast fixing of humankind into just two classes, master-class and slave-class, is not true to the facts. Instead of such social dualism, there is social pluralism, social multiplicity and diversity; there is an indefinite and indeterminate hierarchy of human values.

But here again I impinge upon a problem of world-historical moment, and must forego its discussion.

Meantime, my sense of the worth, the greatness of Nietzsche, remains. The world needs him as never before. His religion is the religion of life, of beauty, of strength, and must not perish from the earth.

Zarathustra gathers round him in his hut in the mountains a few disciples, among whom is the Most Hideous of Men, he who represents all the woes and tears and sufferings of humanity, he who has slain God by the very hideousness of his sores. And Zarathustra expounds to these his gospel of beauty, his ideal of Superman, his vision of life as it should be, as it can be, redeemed, sanctified, glorified by Superman. When Zarathustra finishes his lyric poem, it is the Most Hideous of Men, the representative of everything that life contains most supremely ugly, who speaks first:

And meanwhile all of them, one after another, had come out into the fresh air and the cool calm night; Zarathustra himself led the Most Hideous of Men by the hand, so that he might show him the beauties of the night and the big round moon and the silvery waterfall by his retreat. There they at last stood silent together, all these old men, but their heart was comforted and full of courage, and they wondered secretly that it could be so pleasant on earth; but the stillness of the night pressed ever more deeply upon them. And again Zarathustra thought to himself: "Oh, how they do please me, these superior men"; but he did not give expression to his thought, for he respected their happiness and their silence.

But then happened this most astonishing event of that long and astonishing day; the Most Hideous of Men began once more and for the last time to gurgle and to stutter, and when at last he succeeded in speaking, behold! there proceeded a question, clear and decided, from his lips, a clear profound question which moved all those who stood by.

"My friends," said the Most Hideous of Men, "what think you? For the sake of this one day, *I* am for the first time satisfied that I have lived my life. . . .

"It is good to live on earth. One day, one festivity with Zarathustra, have taught me to love the world.

"Was *this*—Life?" I will ask of Death, "Then—again!"

"My friends, what think you? Will you not say unto Death even as I have said: Was *this*—Life? For the love of Zarathustra, then, once more!"

So Zarathustra—it is the great victory—has taught even the Most Hideous of Men to love life. And under the impression caused by this confession of the Most Hideous of Men, of him who has slain God, the assembled little group of disciples to whom Zarathustra has revealed its secret, break forth into that exquisite song, sung to the accompaniment of the church bell ringing in the solemn hour of midnight—the hour which marks the end of the old day and the dawn of the new:

One!
O Man! Give heed!
Two!
What saith the midnight deep!
Three!
I slept in sleep——
Four!
From deepest dream I wake;
Five!
The world is deep,
Six!
And deeper than the day can know,

> *Seven!*
> Deep is its woe——
> *Eight!*
> Joy—deeper than affliction still,
> *Nine!*
> Who saith: Begone!
> *Ten!*
> But all Joy wills Eternity——
> *Eleven!*
> Wills deep, profound Eternity!
> *Twelve!*

Thus spake Zarathustra. Then took he his eagle and his serpent, and sprang up the rocky way to the Alpine summit, first to be smitten by the sun of the new morning.

Peering through the night, at length he cried: "The Sun! The Sun! The Sun!"

CHAPTER THIRTEEN

NIETZSCHE AND JESUS

WITH the exception of his unfinished pamphlet, *The Eternal Recurrence,* no book of Nietzsche is free from criticism of the effects of Christian virtues. Even in his early academic essays, his religious antipathy was present. In *Human, all-too-Human* we find him well launched upon his campaign. But it is in *Antichrist* that we find the flowering of all those antichristian ideas which crop up continually throughout his eighteen volumes. It is in this work that all his earlier conclusions and arguments are drawn together into a compact and complete whole—the most ruthless and deadly assault that any religion of any race of men has ever experienced. In his later great work, *The Will to Power,* Nietzsche returns to this subject, but adds, I think, nothing essentially new to his former treatment. *Antichrist,* then, gives us the substance of his entire contention.

It would be interesting to try to depict the religious history of Nietzsche's soul. It was pointed out in the first chapter that Nietzsche was the son of a Lutheran pastor, and was brought up amid the influences of a religious circle. But no man ever broke away more completely from the environment of his youth. He was himself at first destined for the clerical profession. We have

some fragments, dating from his boyhood, in which we can recognize the natural outlook of coming village *Pfarrer*. For instance, "May God always have me in his keeping!" he wrote before he had left school. And in his first years at the university he drew up a list of the sciences which he aspired to know, "especially," he says, "religion, the solid foundation of all knowledge." But his youthful devoutness changed into a burning hatred, to which, so far as I know, the history of thought furnishes no parallel.

And yet, all his life, Nietzsche was a profoundly religious man. Just as he is an egoist on account of his altruism, an immoralist owing to the strength of his moral conscience, so he was an atheist by religion. His atheism resolves itself into a faith which is as a burning flame, and which glows like the evening star in the pale azure sky. Zarathustra's faith—faith in life, faith in the infinite possibilities of life—this is a faith that shall remove mountains. Yes, Nietzsche was inveterately incurably religious. So he confirms a law which operates everywhere; namely, that religion, under one form or another, is a sociological necessity. We have no single instance, in either practice or theory, of a society without religion. Religion does not necessarily imply belief in a God, that is, in an anthropomorphic deity. What is religion? Religion means the belief of a community, belief in a common ideal, based on identity of interests. All the philosophies apparently hostile to religion are based on religious belief. Would the French Revolution ever have accomplished its purpose if, above and beyond its crimes and follies, beyond the smoke of the Bastille and the blood of the September massacres, the belief in the universal fraternity of man, and in the possibility of a better life under better condi-

tions, had not actuated its leaders? Was not religious positivism, according to the belief of Auguste Comte, its founder, destined to supplant all religions; and yet did it not end by proclaiming, in default of another, the religion of humanity? Socialists and anarchists of to-day, they who wage war on religion and urge the destruction of all religion, have also their religion, and a religion which yields to none in the spirit of self-sacrifice and devotion which it calls forth in its adherents, a religion which has its martyrs to a cause which they believe to be sacred. Every cause, great or small, heroic or ignoble, right or wrong, must be based on belief. And Nietzsche, with his Zarathustrian faith, and his religion, a religion that burnt him up, the religion of life. He could have used the words of Jesus: I am come to kindle a fire upon the earth, and how am I straitened till it be accomplished!

But now, our question is: If Nietzsche was thus profoundly religious, what is the explanation of his outburst of fury against Christianity, a world-religion hitherto supposed to be the highest and most truly final? Would it be too much to say that Nietzsche adopts every maxim which Christianity repudiates, and reprobates every maxim which Christianity exalts? Did he not preach an ideal that was the exact opposite of the Christian ideal?

A word should be said here by way of parenthesis. We must not allow ourselves to be deceived by a certain literary and emotional exaggeration which is at once an apparent weakness and yet a great asset of Nietzsche's. To illustrate my meaning I will quote a few of his extreme sentences:

"There is not one single buffoonery in the gospels; that alone suffices to condemn a book!"

Again: "One must put on gloves in order to touch the gospels, so as to preserve one's hands from contamination."

Again: "The two greatest plagues of the human race [are] Christianity and alcoholism."

And especially observe this concluding passage in *Antichrist:* "I will write this eternal indictment of Christianity upon every wall. . . . I will use letters which even the blind can see. I denounce Christianity as the One great Curse, as the One Corruption, as the One great Instinct of revenge for which no means are too poisonous, treacherous, and small. I denounce it as the One dying Disgrace of humanity."

Such utterances are, of course, *obiter dicta,* and I shall not allow them to influence my discussion.

Accordingly, to our question: Why did Nietzsche hate Christianity, hate it as no religion was ever hated by a son of man of whom we know? The answer in a nutshell is that he considered Christianity the greatest obstacle to the establishment of his ideal.

This leads to a number of related questions: What is Nietzsche's ideal? What is the Christian ideal? Are they reciprocally exclusive? Which is preferable? What is the new thing in Nietzsche's assault upon Christianity?

Before coming to closer quarters with the subject I must point out the original feature of Nietzsche's attack upon Christianity. For he went about his destructive work from an entirely new angle. Before him three wars had been waged against Christianity. In the first, the metaphysics of Christianity was undermined, corroded. This was the outcome of the Copernican astronomy and the doctrine of evolution, together with the notion of natural law. In

the second attack, the historicity of Christian origins was sapped; what was once treated as historical fact was seen to be miracle, myth, legend, folklore, and the like. The third assault was psychological, giving a natural human explanation of those experiences of conversion, regeneration and illumination which had hitherto been referred to a supernatural, divine origin. Thus, historical Christianity in its metaphysical, historical, and psychological aspects had been theoretically overthrown before Nietzsche's day. Yet, strange to say, Christianity continued to live and flourish like a green bay tree, in spite of all this sapping and undermining. Why was this? It was the merit of Nietzsche to see that *such destructive work had not even touched the citadel of the Christian religion.* As Weinel, a fine German scholar, says, *"Religion ist Weltwertung."* Behind the world and in the world there rules an eternal holy will of love, which we may dare distinguish from the world. And do we dare to lay hold of a supreme overmastering ideal as the one needful for our conduct in the world? Do we dare to see in that ideal the will of the world and the will of a God above the world? Here is the crux of the world historical problem. The life-and-death crisis of Christianity begins, therefore, where its world-evaluation is adjudged to be a vain illusion, where its ideal is declared to be a dishonor and a disfigurement of man and an annihilation of the best in man. The attack of natural science touches only the outworks of Christianity, not at all its soul. But it is precisely the *soul* of this religion that is now being assailed, and Nietzsche was the first to find the Achilles heel here. In the last work of his life, *Ecce Homo,* there is a passage which shows his keen insight into this matter:

Hitherto Christianity has been attacked in a false way, not to say a shy and diffident way. The champions of Christianity have an easy time of it, mere child's play, so long as the morality of Christianity is not felt to be a capital crime against life (*Kapitalverbrechen aus Leben*). The question of the mere truth of Christianity—whether it be as regards the existence of God or as to the historicity of its origin—legends, to say nothing of its Christian astronomy and natural science—is an entirely collateral affair, so long as the question of the worth of Christian morals is not dealt with. Is the morality of Christianity good for anything, or is it a disgrace and an ignominy in spite of all the sanctity of its arts of seduction? There are hiding-places of every kind for the problem of truth. Ultimately, believers can even employ the logic of the most unbelieving to show that they are right, to affirm certain things as irrefutable, as outside the means and realm of refutation. This device is called "Kantian Criticism."

This points to Nietzsche's deep insight into the strategical point. He saw that, despite the scientific denial of the dogmas and miracles of Christianity, despite the biological opposition to the origin of Christian history, the theologian was always able to reply to the denial of Christian truth with the counter-argument of Christian practicability. Did not the destroyers of Christian doctrines and the deniers of Christian history—Spinoza, Darwin, Huxley, Spencer, Strauss, Renan—did not these men endorse and vindicate Christian morals? The reasoning of these men held good so far as the scientific aspects of Christianity went, but the results of Christianity were not involved in these reasonings. The Church, meeting the onslaughts of the "higher criticism," denied the necessity of a literal belief in the gospel records as fact. In a word, the Church asserted that while all antichristian critics might be accurate in their purely scientific and logical conclusions, Christianity itself as a workable code was still efficient and deserving of consideration as the most perfect system of conduct the world had ever known.

Nietzsche, therefore, did not go into the field already ploughed by Feuerbach, Voltaire, Hume, Huxley, Spencer, Paine, and a host of lesser "free thinkers." The preliminary battles in the great Homeric warfare against Christianity had already been won—and had failed. Nietzsche saw the futility of proceeding along historical and scientific lines. He turned his attention to a consideration of the effects of Christian morality upon the race, to an inquiry into the causes of pity-morality, and to a comparison of the moral codes in their relation to the needs of humanity.

The reader will agree that Nietzsche does here put his finger upon the final problem, the real assault to be directed against the Christianity of the present. If Christian morality is outclassed by a higher and purer ideal in the presence of which the Christian ideal loses its luster and pales, then Christianity has definitely declined, and its sickness is, indeed, unto death.

And to this attack gather stout fighters. Here stands Nietzsche, confident that the Christian ideal can be replaced by a better. Here stands Ibsen, the great doubter, who knew man's soul in its secret chambers, and who gave expression to the world of the eternally unuttered. His whole life was drama in which the bitter doubt of the nineteenth century was recapitulated and epitomized,— and found a language out of the heart of the Norwegian poet.

Between Nietzsche, who would write new tables of

values, and Ibsen, who would merely destroy the old tables, stood Björnsen, with a happy and open heart in that fled century of doubt, declaring—what so many had experienced—that Christianity is *Über die Kraft,* its ideal is too much for man, too high and unattainable.

As against all three of these men—and they exhaust the possibilities of doubt—there is growing in our Twentieth Century the haunting wonder as to whether anything else but the Christian Ideal can save human beings from cannibalism and anthropophagy.

But we must now approach the center of the subject. What now is this Nietzschean ideal with which it were well to replace the Christian ideal? I can only summarize it, engaging to present no caricature.

The gist of it is that the Nietzschean ideal is the Greek ideal of life. The Greeks loved beauty, the symmetry of forms, the gracefulness of attitudes; they loved strength and power; they combined beauty, symmetry, strength and power in their Olympian deities. The Greeks were also immortal, in the sense of loving life so as to wish for life eternal, life in all its plenitude, all its possibilities, the *integral* life.

By dint of their strength the Greeks were able to raise themselves above pessimism,—above optimism, too,—to rise to a point where the two were resolved in a higher state. Witness Greek tragedy. This tragedy proclaimed at once the beauty of life, the exuberant power of life, desiring eternity for the realization of its infinite possibilities. This Greek faculty of being able to contemplate with serenity the sufferings and woes of life, proves the strength, physical and moral, of the Greek people. The Greeks did not attempt to conceal the sight of life's sufferings in order to pull themselves into an optimistic conception of life. They did not merely succeed in contemplating life's sufferings with serenity and calm, but they went farther and considered the exhibition of suffering and pain to be essential to the understanding of the real value of life, as a countercheck to an undue optimism. The Greeks went farther still,—they considered the sight of suffering and pain as adding to the value and to the beauty of life. They contemplated suffering and pain in the light of an æsthetic manifestation of the Universal Will, of which all life is but the manifestation. After enjoying the sublimity of the Olympian vision of the beauty, the strength and the eternity of life, the Greeks liked to renew their vigor by going once more to the source of life, which is *suffering*. The Greeks considered this suffering and pain and hideousness as the justification of the Olympian vision; and they considered the Olympian vision as justifying the pain and suffering which accompanied its creation, and as being justified by them. What is the reason of suffering and pain? Their only justification, which is yet the supreme justification, is that suffering and pain incite us to create beauty,—are necessary to the creation of beauty. The pain and suffering which are the accompaniment of the whole world-process are also the material with which beauty and art are created. Through suffering and pain our love of life, as synonymous with beauty and with strength, is intensified. Through them we realize the vision of life in beauty, of life in power, of life exuberant and overflowing with wealth, beauty and power, and needing eternity in order to realize that wealth.

This is Nietzsche's conception of life—that of the

Greeks. Nietzsche is an artist, and as an artist he sees life as a manifestation of beauty; he sees life as synonymous with the Will to Power, of domination. And this Will to Power, realized by the Greeks in their conquering activity in all domains, is itself but the expression of the love of life, of the affirmation of life, of the wish to live and to live wholly.

Having arrived at this point, Nietzsche realized that this conception of life was likely to be criticized as capable of penetrating only the few, the select few. And it is certain that the Dionysian conception of life is the antithesis of a democratic one. The creation of beauty is the work of the élite, and of the élite only.

The strength of mind and body which reveals itself in the ability to contemplate the sufferings of life, as being necessary to the creation of beauty, can be the privilege of but few. That view of life which considers suffering as necessary to the creation of beauty, art as the sole justification of life, and which holds that the greater the suffering, both in amount and in intensity, the better for art, is not likely to be appreciated by that vast majority who are called upon to suffer and to die in order that the minority, the *élite,* may be able to enjoy all the more the contemplation of their artistic creations.

The Nietzschean conception of life presupposes the existence of an *élite,* of a minority, strong and powerful, which dominates the rest of humanity. The justification of a ruling class is the justification of humanity, for it is the duty of the ruling class to create the values which give a value to life, a meaning to life.

Really, Nietzsche's conception of art contains all of Nietzsche. He differs profoundly from Schopenhauer here. For Schopenhauer, art is a means of escaping for a while from the tyranny of the will to live. We negatively cease to desire life for a brief moment, for a while the ardent flame of desire is quenched, and in this quenching of the thirst for life lies the value of art. For Schopenhauer, art is a sedative, a drug. For Nietzsche art is a stimulant. He writes:

But does not art bring with it much that is ugly, hard, questionable—does not art, therefore, *suffer* from life to this extent? But this is the pessimistic view. What does the artist himself say? What does the tragic artist communicate to us about himself? Does he not reveal to us precisely the condition in which one stands without fear before the most mysterious and the most terrible? This condition is in itself of great value; he who knows it honors it above all others. The artist reveals it to us—must do so. Courage and the sentiment of liberty in the face of a mighty enemy, of a dread-inspiring power, of a problem which causes us to tremble— this victorious condition is the one chosen by the artist, glorified by the artist. In the face of tragedy, all that is bellicose in our nature celebrates its saturnalia. He who is suffering, he who seeks suffering, the heroic man, celebrates his own existence in the tragedy; for the sake of this alone does the tragic artist drink the cup of sweet cruelty.

And so Nietzsche goes on and preaches to us the necessity of becoming hardened, of being hard, of inflicting suffering, of being able to witness the most terrible suffering. The truly great man is not he who is full of sympathy for his fellows, but he who is capable of inflicting the cruelest sufferings without heeding the cries of his victims. The greatness of a man is to be measured by his capacity to inflict suffering. It is necessary to harden ourselves, to harden ourselves greatly. Take this from *Zarathustra:*

Why so hard? asked once upon the time the piece of kitchen coal of the diamond. Are we not near relatives?

Why so soft? O my brethren, that is what I ask you: are ye then not—my brethren?

Why so soft, so tender, so conciliatory? Why is such self-denial in your hearts? Such little consciousness of your destiny in your look?

And if ye do not desire to be the messengers of Destiny, how can you hope to—triumph with me?

And if your hardness cannot shine forth and cut and crush, how can ye hope to—create with me?

All creators are hard. And it must be a great joy to you to mold the face of centuries as if it were war.

Joy to write your name on the will of centuries as if on brass,—harder than brass, nobler than brass. That alone which is the hardest is also the noblest.

This new table, O my brethren, I write above you: *Become hard!*

From coal to diamond, iron to steel, clay to granite— there we have it! Nietzsche is an enthusiastic and passionate advocate of life in beauty, in power, in force. His ideal is the Greek ideal, the ideal of Dionysos and Apollo, life at any price, life with all its woes and joys and hopes and fears, worshiped, glorified, cultivated. The Superman as the supreme type incarnates this Dionysian and Apollonian vision of life, incarnates the beauty and purity and symmetry of form, the power and force and strength of the unrestrained and unmoral Will to Power. *Life is fundamentally and essentially unjust and immoral.* Everywhere in life we see inequality; everywhere we see the victory go to the strong. The eliminating of the weak by the strong—this is a necessary condition of life. Man is the only being in nature that has tried to oppose his little inventions to the great law of nature. Man has invented the moral law and set it in opposition to the natural law. But the moral law is simply an expression of lack of vitality. The man who loves life, not in spite of its sufferings but because of its sufferings,—the man who is strong enough to seek the complete realization of life's possibilities, who is prepared to undergo the most cruel martyrdom in order to realize them,—such a man will be above and beyond all moral laws which serve but to hinder and check the integral development of his personality.

Such is Nietzsche's ideal, a message that is distinctly pagan, distinctly Hellenic, distinctly Roman, distinctly that of the Renaissance, distinctly Neronian, distinctly antichristian and antidemocratic.

What wonder that Nietzsche hated Christianity, which he thought preached an anæmic ideal, regarded life as a woe, the earth as a vale of tears—and which he thought glorified the weakest and most abject types of humanity?

Life, a lyrical and enthusiastic affirmation of life—life, beautiful, strong, exuberant,—life manifesting itself in a thousand ways, in plenitude and power! That is Nietzsche's ideal. And everything that tends to pessimism, equality, race-decay hinders its realization.

What, then, hinders its realization? The modern state, a creation of the inferior classes of humanity, designed exclusively to benefit these classes. And science by its glorification of the material to the detriment of the ideal, by the mediocrity of the culture it offers, by the leveling and democratizing influence which it exerts, by being thus an enemy of life in beauty, in plenitude, in power. Woman suffrage hinders, by equalizing the natural inequality of man and woman. The moral law hinders, by subjecting man to a law which is nothing else but the expression of the passions and prejudices of the lower classes.

And especially does Christianity hinder, the greatest obstacle of all, the religion of slaves, by slaves, for slaves. Christ versus Zarathustra? Luther versus Machiavelli? The Jesus idea versus the Napoleon idea? Galilee versus Corsica? Does not Galilee, with its Sermon on the Mount, end in Mount Calvary, with its Cross? But perhaps the logical conclusion of Corsica with its master is St. Helena with its slave! Prussianism may lose its mastership. Treitschke, Bismarck, Bernhardi—do not these masters tell us that they are Christians, though they are at the opposite pole to the ideals of the Nazarene with his mountain sermon?

Back of everything else is the everlasting, heartbreaking question whether the root of this tumultuous, torturing universe is force or love. Is force primary and love a mere transitory by-product? That is the question of questions, the doubt of doubts. And the answer to that question must determine who is to be master of the world, Nietzsche or Christ!

Yet we must allow something in common between Nietzsche and Jesus. Jesus was a revaluator of values. If Socrates was the "gadfly" of Athens, Jesus was the incendiary of the world. "I am come to send fire on the earth." The tragedy on Calvary is the supreme instance of the hatred, on the part of mediocrity and vulgarity of mind, of spiritual distinction. Jesus "lived dangerously." There was no preference in Jesus for self-complacency, for love of ease, for second best, for life at any price, for slipping into a warm nook like some backboneless mollusk. He liked the salt spray of life, stinging and tingling. The Sermon on the Mount is sharp and keen-edged and cuts right down into the world's sophistries and lies. The Sermon on the Mount, with its magnificent paradoxes, finds its true environment and atmosphere, not amid questions of state, of nationality and citizenship, woman suffrage, the vulgar morals and conventions of *bourgeoisie*. It finds its home amid the heights and depths of the soul, at those flashes of crisis when the spirit realizes itself as a pilgrim upon a great adventure, rather than as a citizen of a state, or a member of a nation, or as an advancer of so-called progress and civilization. The ethics of the Sermon on the Mount expresses the conditions of a pilgrim adventure rather than provides legislation for men considered as members of a nation, as citizens of a state.

The *civitas dei* of the first Jesus people was no model township placed in some neat garden plot of life; rather, it was like all things worth living for and dying for and was in greater part unrealized, an invitation and a challenge! Jesus was thinking of bigger things than patriotism, mercantilism, domesticity, science and art and social customs. He was thinking of man's inner world of purity and peace and power and good will, and of what their contraries meant. Yes, in some ways Nietzsche and Jesus would have been good friends. The spirit of the gospel treads always on the brink of high adventures. It is dangerous to accept conventions. It is not only the spirit of revolt which in Nietzsche's phrase "dances on the edge of precipices," but the Christian temper at its most distinctive moments does so, too. "As they followed him, they were afraid." It refuses to walk only along trim paths. It breaks out in unexpected ways. It plunges into Dionysiac dance, with a strange medley of fellow initiates from angels to vagabonds, into the innermost forest depths of reality and power. Deep calls unto deep.

Jesus and Nietzsche were one in saying many splendid things, one in their scorn for phlegm masquerading as patience; one in their trumpet call to struggle with self, with circumstances, with the downward drag of mediocrity; one in their beating up against the wind, "the soul's wings never furled."

But one as the two men were in these respects, Nietzsche misunderstood Jesus in part. That Nietzsche brain on fire, that tortured heart of Nietzsche, touched on the Christ. Saying after saying of Nietzsche has the stern flash of the Gospel paradoxes about it. But, for all that, Nietzsche's proud nature saw in Jesus of Nazareth but a gentle dreamer, and in the Church, a decadent cult akin to Buddhism, in fact, not so good. The teaching of Christ was to Nietzsche but an opium drug, robbing mankind of valor, of the heroic virtues, of the tonic strength of life. Most of all do we have from Nietzsche an indictment of pity, branding sympathy as injurious in its results and as having its origin in feebleness of character.

This, however, is a matter for the succeeding chapter. It is a vast subject in itself, and the central one. For the present we may note that Nietzsche thought well of Jesus in many ways, and even wrote as follows:

In truth, he died too early, this Hebrew who is honored by all the preachers of death by slow means. And it has been a fatality for many since then that he died too soon.

He had no time to know anything beyond the tears and the melancholy peculiar to the Hebrew, and also the hatred of the good and the just—this Hebrew Jesus; and suddenly he was seized with the longing for death.

Why did he not remain in the desert, far from the good and the just? Perhaps he would then have learned to live and to love life—and also to laugh!

My brethren, believe me, he died too soon; himself would have retracted his doctrine had he lived to my age! He was noble enough to be able thus to retract.

Thus yet again spake Zarathustra—and Himself went back alone into the desert, and underneath a cold, clear sky he searched the beauty of the blue above him for the bright and morning star!

CHAPTER FOURTEEN

NIETZSCHE AND ATHEISM

DURING the period of the Church's "revelation theology," it was held that man needed God to satisfy intellect, will, and feeling. Or, rather, it was held, not so much that God should satisfy man, as that man should satisfy God: man's chief need was to be needed by God.

Modern functional theology began with Descartes. Descartes' supreme desire was the satisfaction of his *intellect* with *indubitable knowledge*. The God-thought then became to him a necessary auxiliary construction as he demonstrated the actuality of the world. That is, Descartes needed the thought of God, since otherwise he would lose the concept of truth. Other thinkers followed, like Malebranche and Berkeley, to whom the God-idea was of functional importance in their theory of vision, or perception. In general, it was the satisfaction of the cognitive interest which led English theology of the period to think of God primarily as cause. But, owing, for one thing, to the notion of natural law, which explained the phenomena of nature through binding them all together, without calling for the intervention of any force existing outside them—and owing, for another thing, to man's rejection of authority and of donations of knowledge in his business of knowing, the help of the God-idea in cognitive activity was at length dispensed with.

This rational type of functional theology was succeeded by another type, according to which belief in God functioned in satisfying man's volitional and emotional needs: so Pascal, who derived even science from the need of the heart, instead of religion from the need of the intellect. So, too, even Hobbes, who held that the task of theology was not to describe God, or to produce an ontology of God, but to tell us how we may so conceive God as to be able to worship him. That is, theological propositions arise from the will, not to know, but to worship. And these propositions are true if, and only if, they satisfy the will to worship. Thus Pascal and Hobbes anticipated Kant and Schleiermacher.

English theology thought of God rather as *Cause;* the Germans were inclined to think of him rather as *Ideal.* Kant arrived at the concept of the world without the thought of God, and treated the causal category under the head of cosmology. If science dispensed with the service of God in the business of knowing, Kant dispensed with the service of God in both knowing and doing. Kant passed from a *theonomous* ethic to an *autonomous* ethic, much as his theology is called "moral theology." In a word, not only the scientific, but the ethical task of man is accomplished by man alone without God. The moral law is of man, by man, for man. In the interest of the autonomy of reason, man of himself must care for his morality no less than for his science. But man's desire for happiness remains, and for that man cannot care—nor ought he to, since he ought to will morally. Hence the rational wish arises that some being might exist who should *originate our happiness and should affiliate a happy destiny to the moral will.* And hence—not the proof—

but the rational postulate of a God who shall supply happiness to the moral correctness of our wills. Here we have the reduction of God to the function of making man happy.

Schleiermacher aimed at a synthesis of the new religiousness of Kant with the religion of the New Testament and the Reformation. Schleiermacher proclaimed a Kantian Christianity or a Christian Kantianism. According to Schleiermacher God is not a *Denknotwendigkeit*, as the rationalists had said, but a *Gefühlnotwendigkeit*. God, moreover, is not known but felt.

Feuerbach connects with this notion of the emotional necessity of the God-idea. He treats the God-idea, theology, as a branch of anthropology. God has no objective existence as real—but is at most the embodiment of man's ideal. Man is central, not God. What man is worth, so much and no more is his God worth. Consciousness of God is man's self-consciousness; knowledge of God is man's self-knowledge. God, for Feuerbach, is the personification of man's highest thoughts—a beneficent, not an injurious illusion.

We see, then, what has happened in the history of thought. In the old revelation-theology or authority-theology of the Church, God was Creator, Preserver, Savior and Judge—the whole soul's everlasting portion. This *Church* theology was first replaced by a *rational* theology, which said man needs God to help him think and know with certainty. Next this *rational* theology was replaced by a *moral* theology, which said man knows without God's help, but still needs God that he may will virtuously and live happily. In turn, *moral* theology was replaced by *romantic* theology, which said man must both know certainly and will morally without the help of God; the moral law must freely originate from man's will and be freely obeyed by man's will, otherwise man is not a free moral agent at all. Still, man needs so much of God as the old Providence faith expressed. If we do our duty we ought to be happy, and we need God to care for our happiness, since our happiness depends upon circumstances over which we have no control. Thus, the *théodicée* of Schopenhauer and Von Hartmann took up the happiness question,—Schopenhauer holding that this is the worst possible world; Von Hartmann that it is the best possible world, but that it is worse than none; and both denying the possibility of happiness and affirming radical pessimism.

Thus, the reduction of the functional importance of God is complete, since he is excluded from man's life of knowing, willing and feeling. But if a thing is what it does, if that which does nothing is nothing, this negation of the necessity of God is tantamount to the negation of the reality of God.

What then was left but for a Nietzsche to come, and to preach the self-dependence and self-sufficiency of man in truth and goodness and happiness,—although he did not think that happiness was of much importance, caustically remarking: "I do not seek my happiness, I seek my work; only an Englishman seeks his happiness."?

"The greatest modern event," writes Nietzsche, "is this, that God is dead; yet those who know it go on precisely as if nothing had happened."

How did Nietzsche come to know it?

Let us remind ourselves of his early doubt of orthodoxy. Deussen writes of both himself and Nietzsche at

Pforta as follows: "A certain faith remained with us until after our leaving examination, although it was really unconsciously sifted by the excellent methods of historical criticism with which the ancients were treated at Pforta, and which in those days was quite naturally extended to the domain of Biblical literature."

This same Deussen was speaking to Nietzsche on one occasion of the *Life of Jesus* which Strauss had just then published in a new edition, and expressing approval of the book. Nietzsche quickly replied: "The question is important; if you sacrifice Jesus, you must also sacrifice God."

Later, his sister wrote him as follows: "One must always seek truth at the most painful side of things. Now one does not believe in the Christian mystery without difficulty. Therefore, the Christian mysteries are true."

Nietzsche at once replied in a letter which showed the unhappy condition of his mind:

Do you think that it is really so difficult to receive and accept all the beliefs in which we have been brought up, which little by little have struck deep roots into our lives, which are held as true by all our own kith and kin, and a vast multitude of other excellent people, and which, whether they be true or not, do assuredly console and elevate humanity? Do you think that such acceptance is more difficult than a struggle against the whole mass of habits, waged in doubt and loneliness, and darkened by every kind of spiritual depression, nay more, by remorse; a struggle which leaves a man often in despair, but always loyal to his eternal quest, the discovery of the new paths that lead to the True, the Beautiful, and the Good?

What will be the end of it all? Shall we recover those ideas of God, the world and redemption, which are familiar to us? To the genuine seeker, must not the result of his labors appear as something wholly indifferent? What is it we are seeking? Repose and happiness? No, nothing but truth, however evil and terrible it may be.

So are the cross-roads of men marked. If you desire peace of soul and happiness, believe! if you would be a disciple of truth, inquire!

And so Nietzsche went on into his painful and lonely life. At Berlin for a few days, he heard an old, unhappy man say: "Prussia is lost; the liberals and the Jews have destroyed everything with their babblings . . . they have destroyed tradition, confidence, thought itself."

A little later, at the University of Bonn, we find Nietzsche reading ravenously Schopenhauer's *The World as Will and Idea*. And this ended Nietzsche's faith in God. Through all the changes in his thought, his atheism remained the constant factor throughout his life.

In that book, Schopenhauer describes a formidable world. No providence guides it; no God inhabits it; inflexible laws draw it in chains through time and space; laws, however, to which its eternal essence is indifferent, —a stranger to reason. Only blind Will urges us into life, a Will that does not will better goals to the world; a Will that does not will the perfecting and spiritualizing of culture; a Will that does not will the ethicizing and ennobling of humanity; a blind Will that wills no goal, but wills merely willing, living, willing itself, affirming itself. It nourishes itself upon itself, since outside of it there is nothing, and since it is a famished Will. It tortures itself, therefore, and suffers. Life is desire, desire is an unending torment. The good souls of the Nineteenth

Century believe in the dignity of man, in progress. They are dupes of a superstition. This Primal Will ignores men —the "last comers on the earth, who live, on an average, thirty years." Progress is a stupid invention of the philosophers, under the inspiration of the crowd. Will, an offense to reason, has neither origin nor end; it is absurd, and the universe which it animates is without sense.

Friedrich Nietzsche read greedily the two thousand pages of this metaphysical pamphlet. For fourteen days he scarcely slept. He went to bed at two o'clock, rose at six, spent his days between his book and his piano. His soul was full to the brim. It had found its truth. That truth was hard, but what matter? For a long time his instinct had warned and prepared him for this.

There was that letter to his sister: "What do we seek? Is it repose or happiness? No, truth alone, however terrible and evil it may be." He recognized the somber universe of Schopenhauer. He had had presentiments of it in the reveries of his boyhood, in his readings of Æschylus, of Byron, of Goethe.

In his last book, *Ecce Homo,* referring to his essays published as *Thoughts out of Season,* we find this important statement: "The essays made him [one Professor Hoffmann] foresee a great future for me; namely, that of bringing about a sort of crisis and decisive turning point in the problem of atheism, of which he recognized in me the most instinctive and most radical advocate. It was atheism that had drawn me to Schopenhauer."

But the implication of the wording of this sentence is that Nietzsche was already inclined to atheism; already, in a measure at least, atheistic. That Nietzsche felt deeply and painfully this loss of God—that there was nothing

[221]

flippant, boastful, supercilious, or arrogant in connection with this experience, is evident from the fact that in all his works he speaks of the death of God as the most noteworthy event in the whole history of humanity, as the most formidable overthrowing in the history of human existence. The sense of loss that his loss of God cost him breathes in his words when he says, as quoted by his sister in the *Zukunft,* October 2, 1897: "A deep man has need of friends—unless he still has his God." Few things in Nietzsche's writings have impressed me more than the discourse of a madman running about in the clear daylight, lantern in hand, looking for God. This discourse appears in *Joyful Wisdom:*

"Where is God?" he cried. "I will tell you. We have killed him, you and I! We are all his murderers! But how did we do it? How did we drink the ocean? Who gave us the sponge to wash off the entire horizon? What did we do when we separated this earth from its sun? Whither is it traveling now? Whither are we traveling? Away from all suns? Do we not keep moving continuously? Backwards, sideways, forward, in every direction? Is there still a height and a depth? Are we not wandering toward everlasting annihilation? Do we not perceive the indications of this immense void? Is it not colder? Is not the night becoming darker and darker? Must we not light our lanterns at noon? Do you not already hear the noise of the grave-diggers who are burying God? Do you not already smell the putrefaction of the Almighty?—for even the gods decay! God is dead! God will remain dead! And we have killed him! How shall we be consoled for this, we murderers of murderers? He whom the world held to be most sacred and most powerful has bled on our knives—who shall wash the stain of this blood from us? In what water can we be purified? What form of expiation must we invent? Is not the very greatness of this act too great for us? Must not we ourselves become Gods to seem worthy of it? Never before was so great a deed performed—and all those born after us, will by that very fact, belong to a higher form of history than has hitherto existed!" At this point the madman stopped speaking, and looked at his hearers again. They, too, were silent, and looked at him uneasily. At last he flung his lantern on the ground, where it broke in pieces and went out. "I am here too early," he said. "The time has not yet come. This dreadful event is still on its way, it is approaching; but it has not yet reached the ears of men. Time is needed for people to see and understand thunder and lightning, the glow of the stars, and deeds, even after they have been accomplished. This deed lies farther from you than the farthest constellations—*and yet you yourselves performed it!*"

In saying that Nietzsche felt the loss of his God, it must not be supposed that his rupture was an act of revolt, or that it involved violence or laceration of spirit. Nor must it be supposed that a sad and depressing sense of loss lasted throughout his life. On the contrary, he writes again in *Joyful Wisdom:*

We philosophers and "free spirits" feel ourselves irradiated as by a new dawn by the report that "the old God is dead"; our hearts overflow with gratitude, astonishment, presentiment, and expectation. At last the horizon seems open once more, granting even that it is not bright; our ships can at least put out to sea in face of every danger; every hazard is again permitted to the discerner; the sea, *our* sea, again lies open before us; perhaps never before did such an "open sea" exist.

Indeed, it is not long until Nietzsche is not only reconciled to the loss of God, but assumes an uncompromising attitude of bitterness and scorn toward the concept of God, especially toward the God-idea of the Christian.

Take this passage:

The Christian concept of God—God as the deity of the sick, God as spider, God as spirit—is one of the most corrupt concepts of God that has ever been attained on earth. Perhaps it represents the low-water mark in the evolutionary ebb of the Godlike type. God degenerated into the *contradiction of life,* instead of being its transfiguration and eternal *yea!*

Or this other passage:

An omniscient and omnipotent God who does not even take care that his intentions shall be understood by his creatures,—could he be a God of Goodness? A God who for thousands of years has permitted innumerable doubts and scruples to continue unchecked as if they were of no importance in the salvation of mankind, and who, nevertheless, announces the most dreadful consequences for anyone who mistakes his truth,—would he not be a cruel God if, being himself in possession of the truth, he could calmly contemplate mankind, in a state of miserable torment, worrying its mind as to what was truth?

Or, once more, take this mocking passage:

He was a hidden God, full of secrecy. Verily he did not come by his son otherwise than by secret ways. At the door of his faith standeth adultery. When he was young, that God of the Orient, then he was harsh and revengeful and built himself a hell for the delight of his favorites. At last, however, he became old, and soft, and mellow, and pitiful, more like a grandfather than a father, but most like a tottering old grandmother. There did he sit shriveled in his chimney-corner, fretting on account of his weak legs, world-weary, will-weary, and one day he suffocated of his all-too-great pity.

And so God is dead! And Nietzsche would accept none of the historical traditional substitutes for this God that died. He repudiated world-ground, First Cause, Spinozistic Substance, moral order of the world, especially the modern deification of nature. He would have no vaporization of God into pure spirit, or system of values. He did not believe in our humanizing and teleologizing and ethicizing of nature. Nature was nature, not man with a conception of the distinction between right and wrong, good and evil. He warned us to be on our guard in speaking of the universe as either an organism or a mechanism —words which, by implication, point to a pale survival of the old God that is dead. He was particularly severe in criticizing those who retained what he called shadows of God.

No,—God, the whole God, was dead. And Nietzsche would have no pale, feeble, degenerate God of the palest of all pale persons, the metaphysicians—metaphysicians to whom God himself had become a spider and a metaphysician. Nietzsche had peculiar scorn for this God ever becoming thinner and paler, becoming now an Ideal, now a thing-in-itself, now a pure spirit,—an Absolute. To him all this is but the downfall of a God!

What now was the ground of Nietzsche's atheism? Did he reject theism because it had been logically refuted, and accept atheism because it had been logically proved? I do not so understand it. His renunciation of God was instinctive rather than rational. Instead of disproving God, Nietzsche shows how the idea was originated. "The concept of 'God,'" he writes in *Ecce Homo,* "was invented as the opposite of the concept life—everything detrimental, poisonous, and slanderous, and all deadly hostility to life, was bound together in one horrible unit in Him." And he adds: "The concepts 'beyond' and 'true world' were invented in order to depreciate the only world that exists—in order that no goal or aim, no sense or task, might be left to earthly reality." God ceased to exist because life and history had repudiated Him. God passes as a building crumbles; as summer passes into autumn and autumn into winter; as the sun slowly descends the evening sky and goes down behind the mountain or beneath the waves of the sea. Not logic, but life, which does not need God, lets him go. Nietzsche, with his intellectual skepticism, has scant respect for logic, for he says that a thing that can be proved cannot be of much value.

Indeed, as Lichtenberger remarks, Nietzsche—a profoundly religious man, if by religion we mean the cult of the ideal—was an atheist by religion. Perhaps that is why he was an atheist without despair and without moral anxieties. In a striking passage in *Joyful Wisdom,* he declares:

We can see what in reality vanquished the Christian God; it was Christian morality itself, the notion of sincerity applied with an ever-growing rigor; it was the Christian conscience, sharpened in the confessionals, which transformed and sublimated itself to the point of becoming the scientific conscience, the intellectual "clean linen" desired at all costs.

Referring again to Lichtenberger, the reader will be interested in his fine analysis of the situation:

Nietzsche's religious fervor [he writes] was really directed to the "God of Truth," and when he gradually came to perceive that he must choose between "God" and "Truth," he remained in reality faithful to his religious instinct by sacrificing an historic and traditional belief to a profound inner conviction. And this conviction, of which we know the final origin, was and remained the guiding star of his entire thought and life; for Nietzsche did not separate his life from his thought, and *lived* his atheism as he had formerly *lived* his Christianity. Urged on by this all-powerful instinct of intellectual sincerity, he demolished, stone by stone, the whole edifice of the old world founded upon the belief in God. He ceased to believe in the providential goodness and order of Nature, to see in history the proofs of a divine reason and the sign of a moral will guiding the destinies of humanity, to interpret the events of our lives as trials sent by God to put us in the way of salvation. He called in question all the religious beliefs which had consoled mankind for century after century, and all the values which they had recognized. Determined to think his thought out to the utmost limit, he cast doubts upon morals, even upon truth itself; he asked himself up to what point it was right to prefer good to evil, truth to error. And the more he plunged into this state of negation, the more distinctly did he discover the positive end toward which he was tending; and he formulated with an ever-growing clearness his personal and individual reply to the problem of the sense of life: *"All Gods are dead: now we will that the Superman shall live."* By losing his God, Nietzsche discovered himself.

At bottom, it was Nietzsche's new morality of the Will to Power that made all faith in God impossible,—above all, in the Christian God. It seemed self-evident to Nietzsche that the God of the old ideal should go down with that ideal itself. He always tried to make it appear that his atheism was the natural fruit of his new values. The strong, sound man cannot endure that he himself should not be God if there are gods at all. And then:

"Love for just one being is barbarism, since it is thus exercised at the cost of all others,—and this is true of even love to God."

And yet this thought, in *Beyond Good and Evil*, is somewhat neutralized by what Nietzsche says a few pages earlier:

To love mankind for God's sake—this has so far been the noblest and remotest sentiment to which mankind has attained. That love to mankind without any redeeming intention in the background is only an additional folly and brutishness, that the inclination to this "love" has first to get its proportion, its delicacy, its grain of salt and sprinkling of ambergris from a higher inclination:—whoever first perceived and "experienced" this, however his tongue may have stammered as it attempted to express such a delicate matter, let him for all time be holy and respected, as the man who has so far flown highest and gone astray in the finest fashion.

Indeed, Nietzsche, having hard work to keep from loathing man, loved man for Superman's sake, as he here praised the love of man for God's sake.

Yet some of his writings show that Nietzsche came to the conviction that the whole moral life was degraded by faith in God.

The courage of a Christian, of a believer in God, can never be courage without witnesses. . . . What? Never permitted to be alone with one's self? Never unwatched, unshielded, never out of leading-strings, never to be without gifts given to you! Why, if someone else is always with us the best of courage and of goodness in the world is therefore made impossible. Are we not tempted to fly to hell before this continual obtrusiveness of heaven, this unescapable supernatural neighbor? Never mind, it was only a dream; let us wake up!

Nietzsche quotes what a little girl said to her mother. (Theologians have ridiculed this, but I find it worth thinking over.) "Mother is it true that God is everywhere? But I think that is improper!" A hint for philosophers, Nietzsche adds.

That Nietzsche's own idea of the passing of theism is an outcome of history and life may be seen from a suggestive passage in *Beyond Good and Evil:*

Why Atheism nowadays? The father in God is thoroughly refuted; equally so "the judge," "the rewarder." Also his "free will"; he does not hear—and even if he did, he would not know how to help. The worst is he seems incapable of communicating himself clearly; is he uncertain?—This is what I have made out (by questioning and listening at a variety of conversations) to be the cause of the decline of European theism; it appears to me that although the religious *instinct* is in *vigorous growth,* it rejects the theistic satisfaction with profound distrust.

I must now revert to my earlier statement that for English thought God was Cause; for German, Ideal.

To be sure, in a valid concept, most believers would combine Cause and Ideal. I revert to this that I may point out how, in Nietzsche's substitutes for the dead God, the Will to Power takes the place of Divine Causation, the Superman the place of the Ideal.

As to the Will to Power, we have seen that this replaces Schopenhauer's Will to Live. According to Nietzsche the Will to Power is not monistic, but pluralistic, a multiple center of energy. "The world is Will to Power, and nothing else," he says—as seen most clearly in the conduct of men. "The love of power is the demon of mankind," he says.

Nietzsche's favorite simile for the world is that of the sea. "It is energy everywhere, the play of forces and force-waves, at the same time one and many, rising here and falling there, a sea of forces storming and raging, forever changing . . . with an ebb and flow of its forms."

Nietzsche objects to the conception of the world as completely mechanical, or completely rational, or completely providential, or as otherwise predetermined to reach some far-off and final goal—and he so objects because all such views tend to paralyze human effort, to impoverish human life, making human striving either futile or unnecessary. He has a tragic conception of the universe, "false, cruel, contradictory, seductive, and without sense." This conception does not make him a pessimist, but braces him and heightens his conception of human life and destiny.

What Nietzsche wants is a malleable world, a world in the making, a world in which human effort counts for something, in which men are not puppets, either tugged by mechanical wire-pullers, or guided by a divine stage manager. Here, then, we have the real basis of his special horror of the way the conception of God has often been used to the detriment of human life. The world, the flesh, and the devil too, so detested by traditional Christianity, were worth more to life than the Church-God.

Yet I must insist that Nietzsche's philosophy is not entirely Godless. I find that Wollf is approximately right when he says:

Nietzsche combines the immanent pantheistic view of God

with the idea of evolution and eternal recurrence. The resulting conception is that of a becoming God who is identical with the universe *at each culminating stage* of its development in the infinite course of its eternal recurrence. In other words, the universe in the course of its evolution becomes God whenever it arrives at the stage of maximum power, and then ceases to be divine as it begins its course of declining or descending life, until it reaches again its zenith, and so on incessantly.

So Wolff interprets Nietzsche, and we are reminded of Nietzsche's own statement that "God is the culminating moment: life is an eternal process of deifying and undeifying."

This notion of a becoming God is not ungrateful to many contemporary minds, being a notion, it is thought, which tends to enrich life and to stimulate human effort. Such a God and man can be coworkers.

But as to the other God-ingredient, the Ideal, replaced by Superman, I cannot do better than quote *Zarathustra:*

The God who beheld everything, *and also man:* that God had to die! Man cannot *endure* it that such a witness should live.

The beauty of the Superman came unto me as a shadow. Ah, my brethren! Of what account now are—the Gods to me!—

Once did people say God, when they looked out upon distant seas; now, however, have I taught you to say Superman.

The Superman is the meaning of the earth. Let your will say: The Superman *shall be* the meaning of the earth! I conjure you, my brethren, *remain true to the earth!*

Thus spake Zarathustra and left his cave, glowing and strong, like a morning sun coming out of gloomy mountains.

CHAPTER FIFTEEN

NIETZSCHE AND SUPERMAN

"SUPERMAN" translates the German *Ubermensch:*
"Overman," "Beyond-Man." G. Chatterton Hill, Broene,
Dodson, and Paul Carus, protest that "Superman" is a
barbarism, being a hybrid formed of a Latin (*super*) and
an English word (man): They prefer and recommend
"Overman." But "Superman" persists, and is now our
subject, lit up by any light that "Overman" and "Beyond-
Man" can throw upon his sphinxlike face.

For sphinx he seems to be. Superman is the best
known and least understood slogan of the Nietzschean
philosophy. To be sure, the word *Ubermensch* is not original with Nietzsche. Goethe uses it in *Faust,* where the
Earth Spirit mocks the superhumanity of Faust with these
words:

*"Da bin ich! welch erbärmlich Grauen Fasst, Ubermen-
schen, dich!"* Goethe uses it again in a preface to his
poems strikingly applicable to Nietzsche. The word occurs
also in Herder's *Briefe Zu Beförderung Humanität,* and
the meaning offers a striking parallel to Nietzsche's conception of the essence of an aristocratic social order.
"There came a time," writes Herder, "when the word
homo got an entirely different meaning from what it
had with the ancients. *Homo* was a bearer of duty,
an underling, a servant, a vassal. Whoever was not

this enjoyed no rights, was not sure of his life; and those to whom these serving-men belonged were *Ubermenschen*." And again: "Nothing impedes more than unfeeling, proud *hardness*—the idea that one is of higher stock, is entirely different, or *sui generis*. This embitters everyone and brings inevitable evil to *Ubermenschen, viz.*, his heart remains unbroken, empty, and uncultivated; everyone in the end hates him and despises him." So Herder. But from Goethe and Herder to Nietzsche, R. Meyer, who has written a monograph on the word finds it only twice in literature, and having no profound significance at that. Did Nietzsche get the word from these men, or did he use it independently? We cannot be sure. This, too, is sphinx, and not of much importance. What is important is the great question: *Who is this Superman?* Is he superanimal, as some say; or supermaniac, as other cynics say; or is he simply genius, great personality; or a new species which shall replace man? Is he merely a high type of man, or is he a being as far in advance of man as man is of the ape? That is the question.

First of all, we must break a lance with Nietzsche's sister, who was incensed at the interpreters of her brother, —Nietzsche's sister, who frankly admits that she is the only one who understands what he means by "Superman." Despite Peter Gast, I think she largely misunderstands this matter. She was always oversensitive about her brother's sanity and Christianity—and some of his critics think that his Superman clinches the argument against both of these desiderata.

We must first bring out the sister's point for what it is worth. Her point is that Nietzsche meant to set forth a parable which should represent the vast gulf that separates the ordinary mortal from the exceptional genius. She would hold, accordingly, that Superman is merely a high type of man. Now, if Nietzsche had stopped with his first thought on the subject, Lizzie would be right; but he passed on into a second thought, *viz.*, Superman is as different from man as man is from the ape. But Lizzie does not allow this plain meaning of her brother's position, because it involves evolution, which, like an orthodox Lutheran, she dislikes, and she insists that Nietzsche never held to the Darwinian hypothesis. And one can find passages in Nietzsche's writings that support his sister's contentions. In his *Joyful Wisdom* does he not speak of Darwin's incomprehensibly one-sided doctrine of the struggle for life? Does he not go on to say that not *necessity,* but *abundance,* reigns in nature? that the struggle for life is an exception? Does he not even ridicule the Darwinians, saying: "You accept this mediocre Reason of this English joker for 'philosophy'?"

In his *Dawn of Day* Nietzsche declares positively: "However highly mankind may be developed—perhaps in the end it will be on a lower scale than it was in the beginning—a transition to a higher order is no more attainable than the ant and earwig, at the end of 'their earthly career' can aspire to a kinship with God and Eternity."

We could hardly ask for anything more explicit than the following utterance:

The problem I have put is not what is to replace mankind in the chain of beings (man is an *end*) but what type of man we are to *cultivate,* we are to *will,* as the more valuable, the more worthy of life, the more certain of the future.

This more valuable type has often enough existed already, but as a happy accident, as an exception, never as *willed*. . . .

[234]

Mankind does not manifest a development to the better, the stronger or the higher, in the manner in which it is at present believed. "Progress" is merely a modern idea, *i.e.*, a false idea. The European of the present is, in worth, far below the European of the Renaissance; onward development is by no means by any necessity, elevating, enhancing, strengthening.

In another sense there is a continuous succession of single cases in the most different parts of the earth, and from the most different civilizations, in which, in fact, a *higher type* manifests itself; something which, in relation to collective mankind, is a sort of Beyond-Man. Such happy accidents of grand success have always been possible, and will, perhaps, always be possible. And even entire races, tribes, and nations can, under certain circumstances, represent such a good hit.

It may be conceded, then, that Nietzsche was not an unalloyed Darwinian. Nevertheless, as opposed to Nietzsche's sister, no reader of his writings can escape the conviction that he held fundamentally to the hypothesis of evolution—and that is the main thing.

I have to urge, then, first, that Nietzsche uses the word Superman in two senses, *as the highest representative of man,* which his sister allows; but also, as *a new type,* which is to be *the next species above man* in the evolutionary process, an interpretation which his sister does not allow but combats. And I have to urge, secondly, that his sister is wrong in refusing Darwinian leanings on the part of her brother. That the term Superman represents for Zarathustra an idea quite Darwinian, and that the struggle for life and the survival of the fittest are its warp and woof, he who runs may read.

To repeat, Nietzsche uses the word Superman in two senses: first, as meaning *an ideal human being;* and later, as meaning a *supertype,* a species above man. In what sense the word is used in any given case will, of course, depend on the context.

Used in the first sense, as an ideal human being, we find that the term has a long history in Nietzsche's life. When a boy of seventeen at school, reading a paper on Byron's poetry to his literary society, he describes Byron's heroes as supermen, just as he described Shakespeare's heroes twenty years later. "The goal of humanity lies in its noblest specimens"—that was his youthful ideal. He continues it in *Schopenhauer as Educator* when he says: "Humanity must constantly labor to produce great individuals—this is its task and no other."

But, after all, this thought is not strikingly novel. Long ago, the Stoics and Epicureans had their "wise man," their sage; the Renaissance had its *homo universalis;* many moderns have their great "individual," their genius. In the great individual all the movements of the time are recapitulated and epitomized. The great personality is not simply many-sided, he is all-sided—a wonder-work of nature. Such a man was Voltaire. The physiognomy of the Eighteenth Century would be entirely different, if we were to think Voltaire out of it. He cannot be thought out of it. His name is intergrown with that age into an indissoluble unity. He was the genius of work. In battling down superstition in all its forms and shades, Voltaire was fearless to the point of self-immolation. Precepts and revelations; heavenly and earthly despots; written and unwritten laws; crown and cap, mitre and hood; dogmas and systems—none of them seemed imposing to Voltaire. Respect for the wrinkles on the aged brow of history, for the mildew and rust of tradition—this was wholly wanting in Voltaire's make-up. He was the genius and apostle of disrespect. It almost seems as if, to Voltaire, respectability were the only disgrace.

Now Nietzsche's Superman was to have this attitude toward the old table of values, but was also, unlike Voltaire, to be the creator of a new table of values. Superman was not simply to be ruthless iconoclast, but creator of values.

If we turn to the condition of modern Europe which Nietzsche condemned, we shall understand the function of his Superman, in his first sense—of ideal human being.

According to Nietzsche, a striking fact which we witness at present in Europe is the gradual and sure development of a mediocre type of humanity at the expense of the superior races. The gregarious animal, living with and by the herd, has nearly eliminated the solitary individual, strong in his solitude. On the one hand, we see a constant growth of morbid characters as a result of the progress of civilization, notably an enormous increase of nervous diseases. On the other hand, we see a steady growth of mediocrity, a growth nurtured alike by the modern state and by modern science. Growth of mediocrity and degeneracy! Yet, according to Nietzsche, interestingly enough, these are not to be condemned in themselves. The growth of mediocrity is a necessary condition for the establishment of a superior race, of a race of masters. History teaches us that the ruling races have invariably a very limited existence. The aristocracy of Athens decayed in two hundred years, and yet Athens was comparatively peaceful. The duties of the *élite* are in themselves of a nature to destroy that *élite* within a short period. Their love of war and adventure, their ambition, decimate the ranks of the superior races. He who is strong and power-ful, and a lover of life, consumes his energy without further thought. The strong man spends out of the over-flowing richness of his vitality. He does not care for a long life—what he desires is the intense life, the integral life, the *maximum* life. Thus, Nietzsche thinks, the existence of a more peaceful, mediocre, and stable type is necessary in order to ensure the survival of the species; for, if the species were exclusively composed of the aris-tocratic and ruling races, it would inevitably die out. Thus the "slaves," the great mass of humanity, mediocre, and uninteresting, must exist as a pedestal for the monument of genius.

But think what a costly process this development of the vast social fabric is! Think what an immense exploitation of human labor it represents! Surely, we must ask what is the value of this exploitation? What is its aim? "The greatest happiness of the greatest number," says the Anglo-Saxon. "Then its aim is low, its value is of no account," replies Nietzsche. This gigantic exploitation of human labor, this complicated social process, must, in order to be justified, find an aim which shall give it ade-quate value. And it can attain adequate value only if its aim be *the creation of a higher race, of a race of con-querors, of masters who shall, by their works, give a meaning to humanity.*

In his *Will to Power*, Nietzsche gives us one of his greatest thoughts:

Can we believe that the increase of the costs borne by every individual will result in an increase of profit? The contrary seems to be true: the individual costs added together produce generally a deficit; man finds himself diminished in value, so that one is at a loss to understand, in the end, the wherefore of this immense evolution. A *Wherefore?* A new Wherefore? That is what humanity most needs.

This exploitation of humanity, which is implied in the maintenance and development of the social structure—what justifies it? Only its aim to create beauty, to create a superior race which shall set the seal of its own value on humanity, and give to humanity ideals for a thousand years hence. The *State* is not an end in itself. *Society* is not an end in itself. State and society are justified only as *substructures* on which the superstructures of the Superman may found itself. The superior race of masters is itself its own justification. It is a luxury of humanity, representing the profit realized on the exploitation of human labor, "concretized" in the social organization. It is a race of rare and tropical plants, of Olympian artists in the full sense of the word, who live in beauty, and who create beauty by their force and intrepidity and plenitude in all spheres of activity.

Lichtenberger rightly defines Nietzsche's first Superman as follows:

The state which man will attain when he has renounced the existing hierarchy of values, and has rejected the Christian, democratic, or ascetic ideals which prevail actually in Europe, and when he has returned to the table of values admitted by the noble races, by the masters, who *create* for themselves their own values instead of receiving them from outside.

But Lichtenberger does not give due weight to the further fact that the conception of the Superman differs from all the philosophical conceptions which have preceded it in that it is essentially the philosophy of a class, and of a very small and limited class. Zarathustra came to preach the Superman, not to humanity, but to the chosen few of humanity, to the superior men who are disgusted with modern ideas and modern civilization. Up in his grotto, in the solitude of the mountains, Zarathustra has collected a number of superior men and has given them hospitality. Let me marshal the group, one by one, before you. Here is the sage who, pessimistically, sees all around him symptoms of decay and death, and who preaches: "All is vanity." Here are two Kings, constitutional Kings, who have abandoned their kingdoms because, being no longer the real chiefs of their subjects, they take no pleasure in the fiction of royalty. Here is the modern scientist, the "objective" thinker, who has devoted his life to a study of the brain-structure of the leech. Here is the magician, the professional politician, who has played every rôle and deceived everyone in turn, but who cannot deceive himself any longer and who seeks in vain a true genius. Here is the Most Hideous of Men, he who has slain God, he who represents all the miseries and sufferings of humanity during its long evolution from the anthropoid to man; God has been slain by the sight of so much hideousness, of so much misery and wretchedness, for God has had to contemplate this work of his unceasingly, and he has contemplated it until he is slain by it. Here is the last of the Popes, unable to console himself for the death of God. Here, also, is the skeptic, he who has partaken of every opinion, of every conviction, in turn, only to abandon each one successively, and, at last, disgusted, faithless, and hopeless, has taken refuge in the solitude of the mountains with Zarathustra. For this poor wanderer of a skeptic Zarathustra is filled with pity. He sees in him the image of his own shadow, for Zarathustra, too, has harbored every conviction, has been tossed about on the stormy sea of life, and knows life in all it brings of illusion, disappointment and deception. And Zarathustra feels the disgust and disappointment of this wandering soul in distress, and has for him some words of profound pity:

Thou art my Shadow, he said with sorrow.

The danger thou dost confront is not small, O free spirit, bold traveler! Thou hast spent a bad day; take care that the night be not worse for thee.

For wanderers like unto thee, a prison itself ends by seeming a welcome refuge. Hast thou seen how quietly and peacefully the imprisoned malefactors sleep? They sleep peacefully, for they enjoy their new security.

Take care, lest in the end, thou shouldst become the slave of a narrow belief, of a hard and rigorous delusion! Henceforth everything which is narrow and solid must prove attractive to thee.

Thou hast lost thy aim! . . . and thus—hast thou lost also thy way!

Poor wandering soul! poor tired butterfly!

Now all these refugees—the sage, the two Kings, the scientist, the Ugliest Man, the skeptic—to whom Zarathustra offers the hospitality of his mountain grotto, are the "superior men" of to-day; they are those "hard skeptical spirits" who are the honor of our time; disgusted with the growing democratization of Europe, having lost their ideals out of their faith and their hope, they are profoundly pessimistic, loathing man and the world and aspiring to nothing but Nirvana. Neither material nor

[241]

ideal satisfaction are henceforth adequate to them. They are the victims of modern culture.

But Zarathustra has not come merely to preach the "great disgust" of man. Zarathustra has come to give humanity "the new Wherefore" which is necessary for its continued existence. Zarathustra has come to preach a new gospel, to give to the world a new aim and a new ideal. And this new aim and ideal is symbolized by the Superman.

But at this point the second meaning of Superman—*supertype*—emerges, and there is a blending of the two. And so at this point we must go back to Nietzsche's peculiar modification of Darwinism, and thus work our way into the heart of his thought.

What is the goal which Nietzsche sets to will—his and ours? Not "usefulness," not pleasure (*Lust*), not happiness (*Glück*)—ours or others'. The ultimate worth is *life.* He wills life *über alles;* he says *Yes* to life—*i.e.,* he appraises life as the highest good. Not simply his own life, but *the* life; the life of the individual is but a wave in the stream of the whole of life,—and it might very well be that this wave must prematurely dash itself against a rock—shed its blood—to create a free path for the whole stream. Nietzsche affirms life in its entire length and breadth and height and depth—*das Leben als das Urprinzip alles Seins und alles Werdens.* And everything which necessarily belongs to life, which preserves and augments life, must be conjointly evaluated. But pleasure *and* pain, usefulness *and* injury, fortune *and* misfortune—all these are indispensable constituents of life itself. And Nietzsche was never weary of repeating how precisely our own injury, how above all the supreme pain, is the most important drillmaster in order to life—how life sucks the greatest strength from the greatest pain. Life, then, with all its pleasure and all its pain is affirmed. *Amor fati*—that is Nietzsche's confession of faith. Thus Nietzsche leaves far behind him all utilitarian, eudemonistic, hedonistic principles of morality. *The original worth which he posits is a biological worth.*

But if we go thus far we have to go farther: Taking counsel of our own heart; hearkening to the basic tendency of our own willing; taking sides in harmony with our will, not against but for life; striving to grade all our valuations according to this new goal, we must make one thing clear to ourselves: namely, *what really is* the life which we will to serve?—and we must do this that we may know how we can serve life, what we will to this end, and how we may evaluate. For the *meaning* of things may not be deduced from the surface of things; meaning is nothing that is self-evident, nothing easily knowable. Hence Nietzsche's great question: *What does life want of me, that I may will what it wants, not cross its purpose, but consciously promote it, facilitate it?*

Nietzsche goes to biological science, and, in this way, to Darwinism for an answer. And what is the answer? All living beings belong to groups which the biologist designates as species. These species do not exist from eternity by God's creative fiat; but they have evolved—partly from one another, partly from common ancestors. All species have a common derivation. This we call the Darwinian doctrine of descent, or evolution. But there is another main point. How was it possible that the highest species, like man, could develop out of the lowest species? Natural selection, says Darwin, like artificial breeding of race horses by man's skill. But natural selection is tied up with the struggle for existence. In this struggle the fit and strong survive, even new species originate, suited to new environment.

Now, what holds good of all living beings, is true for man also. Man, too, has not existed since eternity, but arose as other organisms have originated—arose from lower species. This is the point to which Nietzsche fastens. But Darwin was interested in the *origin* of man, while Nietzsche was interested in the *future* of man. Nietzsche's question was not; where did man come from? but, whither does man go? This is what Nietzsche proposes to answer. If the kingdom of living beings presents a pyramid of species, which have evolved out of one another, man being the provisional apex, is it not probable that the life-tendency of the human species likewise consists in a higher development to another, a different species? From the point of view of the evolution theory, may we not say that the meaning of the ape-life consisted in its developing upward to man-life? In the spirit of Darwin must one not maintain that the *life-meaning of every species is to form a transition from a subspecies to a superspecies?* The life-meaning of humanity, therefore, is to fling a bridge to that new life-form which still reposes in the womb of the future,—that new life-form which has no name of its own as yet,—of which we can know as little as our subspecies knew of us,—whose representatives are supermen, as we men are superapes.

Our previous question is now answered—what does life want of men? It wants of men what it once wanted of our subspecies,—apes, perhaps. Life wants men to supersede themselves, to mount above themselves to Beyond-

Man, to Superman. Who, therefore, posits life as the ultimate goal of willing, must also will the rôle which is assigned to humanity *in* life and *by* life, must will *humanity as a forestage to superhumanity*. He will *will* everything, evaluate everything, seek to promote everything which strengthens the evolution of humanity in this direction of superhumanity, but will also fight everything impeding such evolution.

In one great point man is unlike any other species. No species ever consciously desired, willed, worked for, the rise of its superspecies. It is man's highest prerogative, man's supreme self-immolating duty not to trust to nature blindly to bring in his superspecies,—not to trust that such progress is providential, mechanical, deterministic, automatic, but to work and plan for it. No other species knew its calling; no other species could purposefully work to be a down-going in order to be an on-going. Only to man is it given to interpret the meaning of evolution, to recognize its factors, to diagnose the momentary status of the evolution of a species, and to bend the direction of evolution in the line of the meaning, or against the meaning, of the entire development. Prior to man the water of the river of life flowed in a river bed made for it by natural processes; with man, the river bed must be consciously and purposefully improved by man's own initiative and toil. The greatest of all tasks is thus put into man's hands. And Superman is the supreme biological value that there is for man.

Witness again Zarathustra:

I teach you the Superman. Man is something that is to be surpassed. What have ye done to surpass man?

All beings hitherto have created something beyond themselves: and ye want to be the ebb of that great tide, and would rather go back to the beast than surpass man?

What is the ape to man? A laughing-stock, a thing of shame. And just the same shall man be to the Superman: a laughing-stock, a thing of shame.

Ye have made your way from the worm to man, and much within you is still worm. Once were ye apes, and even yet man is more of an ape than any of the apes.

Even the wisest among you is only a disharmony and hybrid of plant and phantom. But do I bid you become phantoms or plants?

Lo, I teach you the Superman!

The Superman is the meaning of the earth. Let your will say: The Superman shall be the meaning of the earth!

I conjure you, my brethren, remain true to the earth, and believe not those who speak unto you of superearthly hopes! Poisoners are they, whether they know it or not.

Despisers of life are they, decaying ones and poisoned ones themselves, of whom the earth is weary: so away with them!

Once blasphemy against God was the greatest blasphemy; but God died, and therewith also those blasphemers. To blaspheme the earth is now the dreadfulest sin, and to rate the heart of the unknowable higher than the meaning of the earth!

Once the soul looked contemptuously on the body, and then that contempt was the supreme thing:—the soul wished the body meagre, ghastly, and famished. Thus it thought to escape from the body and the earth.

Oh, that soul was itself meagre, ghastly, and famished; and cruelty was the delight of that soul!

But ye, also, my brethren, tell me: What doth your body say about your soul? Is your soul not poverty and pollution and wretched self-complacency?

Verily, a polluted stream is man. One must be a sea, to receive a polluted stream without becoming impure.

Lo, I teach you the Superman: he is that sea; in him can your great contempt be submerged.

"What is the greatest thing ye can experience? It is the hour of great contempt. The hour in which even your happiness becometh loathsome unto you, and so also your reason and virtue.

The hour when ye say: What good is my happiness! It is poverty and pollution and wretched self-complacency. But my happiness should justify existence itself.

The hour when ye say: What good is my reason! Doth it long for knowledge as the lion for his food? It is poverty and pollution and wretched self-complacency!

The hour when ye say: What good is my virtue! As yet it hath not made me passionate. How weary I am of my good and my bad! It is all poverty and pollution and wretched self-complacency!

The hour when ye say: What good is my justice! I do not see that I am fervour and fuel. The just, however, are fervour and fuel!

The hour when ye say: What good is my pity! Is not pity the cross on which he is nailed who loveth man? But my pity is not a crucifixion.

Have ye ever spoken thus? Have ye ever cried thus? Ah, would that I had heard you crying thus!

It is not your sin—it is your self-satisfaction that crieth unto heaven; your very sparingness in sin crieth unto heaven!

Where is the lightning to lick you with its tongue? Where is the frenzy with which ye should be inoculated?

Lo, I teach you the Superman: he is that lightning, he is that frenzy!

Yet, Superman is not the goal of life—life will surpass Superman—but Superman is the goal of man.

We must close this discussion with brief mention of a point or two.

(1) For one thing, the Superman will differ profoundly from the "modern man"—having higher qualities which modern men lack: Will to Power, independence, self-confidence. An aristocrat, he frowns on democracy and mediocrity, and believes in the *"pathos of distance."* His code of morality and honor is an aristocratic code, a code for supermen—not for rabble—and not to be popularized. The virtue of the Superman is the virtue of the Renaissance, terrible and fraught with danger for the masses. Superman morality is the *immorality of nature.*

(2) Again, Superman does not regard truth with the superstitious awe of the rest of mankind. Truth is simply an instrument in the struggle for life—there is no such thing as "truth-in-itself"—truth is simply an instrument of power. Knowledge is a means of acquiring power.

(3) For still another thing, what are the means best adapted to the cultivation of Superman, of the superior race of the future? Great suffering is necessary. Here is a beautiful passage from Nietzsche:

It is in the school of suffering—of *intense* suffering—that has been created every great thing that humanity has produced. This tension of the soul which stiffens itself under the load of misfortune, and thus learns to become strong; this shudder which seizes it in the face of a great catastrophe; its ingenuity and courage in supporting, interpreting, utilizing misfortune; and everything which the soul possesses of deepness, mystery, dissimulation, wisdom, ruse, greatness: is not all this acquired in the school of suffering, modeled and cast by great suffering?

This Superman-creator must be "hardened, broken, torn, purified by fire and sword"; he must of necessity suffer. The Superman must be disciplined, and rigidly disciplined.

Nietzsche is not soft-hearted for those who would be his disciples. "I wish those who interest me in one way and another," he says, "I wish them every suffering, isolation, illness, opprobrium. I wish that they may have personal experience of the deepest self-disgust, of self-torture and self-defiance, of the great distress of defeat. I have no pity for them, for I wish them the only thing which can prove whether or not they possess any real value,—*that they hold good.*"

(4) Still again, the Superman must not only have the courage to bear great suffering; he must not only have the courage to seek great suffering and be able to love great suffering as being that which is noblest on the earth; he must also be able to *inflict* great suffering. Nietzsche asks:

Who can hope to attain anything great, if he does not possess sufficient strength and force of will to be able to inflict great suffering? To be able to suffer is the least of things; weak women and even slaves can surpass themselves in that. But not to succumb to a feeling of distress and uncertainty when one inflicts great suffering and listens to the shriek of the sufferer—that is great, that is true greatness.

According to Nietzsche, then, the capacity to inflict great suffering without listening to the cries of the victim is what is really great in a man's character.

Finally, the essence of Superman is that he is true to nature—that he returns to nature. The systems of morals which humanity has set up one after another are all of them systems contrary to nature. The great law of life is: *"Live wholly; live fully!"* This law the Superman realizes. The sentiment actuating Superman is always the sentiment of the Will to Power. Indeed, Superman is the incarnation of the Will to Power under its noblest aspects. It is that Will to Power which pushes him to seek for the realization of life in all its integrity; for only in the measure that we can afford to live fully, to be extravagant and thriftless with our vital power—only in that measure are we strong and powerful.

Thus spake Zarathustra to the superior men that had come to his grotto, and then Zarathustra clambered down the mountain with the rainbows and bridges of the Superman in his hands, to the shore, and turned his ship's prow to distant lands in distant seas—away from Vaterland to Kinderland; he ceased to coast along the shore and quickly set sail for the high seas, eager to do battle with the midnight hurricane!